SUPPORTING
Life

THE CASE FOR A PRO-LIFE ECONOMIC AGENDA

by Michael D. Greaney

Foreword by Rev. Edward C. Krause, C.S.C, Ph.D.

© 2010 Center for Economic and Social Justice

Economic Justice Media

© 2010 Center for Economic and Social Justice

Published by Economic Justice Media, an imprint of CESJ
P. O. Box 40711, Washington, D.C. 20016, U.S.A.
(Tel) 703-243-5155 · (Fax) 703-243-5935
(Eml) thirdway@cesj.org · (Web) www.cesj.org

International Standard Book Number: 978-0-944997-05-5

Library of Congress Control Number: 2009913318

Cover design by Rowland L. Brohawn

Table of Contents

Foreword

Although our graduations are separated by time, and our colleges by subject, both the author of this book and I are graduates of the University of Notre Dame du Lac in South Bend, Indiana. We are connected in other ways as well. We both write for *Social Justice Review*, the editorship to which I succeeded on the death of our mutual friend, the late and very much lamented Father John H. Miller, C.S.C., S.T.D. In addition, we both serve on boards of the Center for Economic and Social Justice ("CESJ"), a non-profit think tank in Arlington, Virginia; I on the Board of Counselors, and Mr. Greaney on the Board of Directors.

Mr. Greaney and I share something else: a concern for the integrity and reputation of our alma mater. Both of us believe this may have been seriously damaged in May of 2009. It was then that Father John Jenkins, C.S.C., president of Notre Dame, bestowed an honorary degree on U.S. President Barack Obama following the issuance of a directive that no Catholic university was to bestow honors on politicians supporting a right to abortion.

Whatever your opinion of Father Jenkins's action, this book responds to Mr. Obama's call during his speech at Notre Dame for "common ground" on which Pro-Life and Pro-Choice adherents can meet and come to some peaceful resolution. I believe that Mr. Greaney's suggestions in this regard merit serious consideration. By "common ground," of course, we mean a common acceptance of the basic principles on which society is based. It does not mean that we necessarily accept someone else's interpretation or application of those principles — that is where the debate occurs, in the realm of politics, not morals.

Mr. Greaney's analysis is divided into five parts. The first part is an examination of the natural law as the

foundation of a just social order. The second part is an
admitted amateur's opinion of the constitutionality of the
right to an abortion established by *Roe v. Wade* viewed
from within the natural law context that provides the basis of the U.S. government. The third takes the presumed
right of choice and draws some logical conclusions. The
fourth part introduces us to what many people might consider a new way of looking at social action: social justice.
The fifth part offers a possible Pro-Life economic agenda
to remove many of the root causes of the conflict.

The third part of this book is based on what some people may regard as a dangerous concession to the Pro-
Choice position: the acknowledgment that the United
States Supreme Court considers abortion a constitutionally protected right. As a professor of moral philosophy,
"ethics," I can assure anyone troubled by these or similar
considerations that acknowledging reality in no way violates a "well-formed conscience," nor in any way constitutes a concession.

On the contrary, St. Thomas Aquinas — considered a
"sure guide" by the Catholic Church and whose Aristote-
lianism is shared by the Jewish philosopher Moses Maimonides and the Islamic scholar Ibn Khaldûn — tells us
that we must accept and obey even the most egregiously
unjust law if we personally are not forced to do that which
we regard as evil, and if the result of disobedience or even
changing the law would seriously disrupt the social order.

We cannot, however, stop there. The social doctrine of
Pius XI as analyzed by Father William Ferree refines our
understanding of the proper course of action in the face of
injustice. When society is badly organized — and unjust
laws are certainly evidence of that! — and correcting the
situation is beyond our individual capacities, there is recourse. That is to organize with like-minded others and
work to reform the institutions of the common good. Once
we have reformed our institutions by means of these acts
of "social virtue," acts of individual virtue become possi-

ble. The goal of social justice is not to replace individual virtue, but to enable it.

Nor can we stop there, either. We must replace bad or defective institutions with institutions better adapted to assist each human being to acquire and develop virtue, that is, to become more fully human. Traditionally, within civil society our capacity to acquire and develop virtue, as well as the best protection for each person's inalienable rights to life and liberty, has been access to the means of acquiring and possessing private property in the means of production. Our growing dependency on the State and our acquiescence in unjust laws and institutions will only be broken when each human person can become an owner not only of his or her own labor, but of capital as well.

I should make it clear that CESJ is not a Catholic, nor even a religious organization. CESJ was founded to promote understanding of the social doctrine of Pope Pius XI and the economic justice principles of Louis O. Kelso and Mortimer J. Adler. The former is as analyzed by Father William J. Ferree, S.M., Ph.D., a CESJ co-founder, while the latter provides the basis for "binary economics." Both are founded on the inherent dignity of the human person before God. Economic and social justice are essential supports of individual sovereignty, albeit realized within a social context. Human dignity and personal sovereignty are both based solidly on the natural law, the principles of which are common to all the great religions and philosophies.

Read this book and reflect on its proposals, with special emphasis on "Capital Homesteading." Then consider in what way you might be able to assist in advancing this "Just Third Way" beyond both capitalism and socialism. A visit to the website of the Center for Economic and Social Justice, www.cesj.org, would be a good place to start.

Rev. Edward Krause, C.S.C., Ph.D.
Professor of Moral Philosophy
Gannon University, Erie, Pennsylvania

The Question

Is there common ground on which Pro-Life and Pro-Choice[1] adherents can meet and discuss the issue of abortion in an atmosphere of mutual respect, solidarity, and compassion? The American economy is a system on terminal life support. It is fueled by annual deficits, growing debt — government and consumer — and redistribution through the tax system. Is it possible to organize to transform the economy to a system that provides equal economic opportunity for all, so that anyone who wishes can become an owner of capital as well as labor — an economy that supports life?

We think so. We believe that an economic agenda based on the natural moral law provides part of that common ground. The rest is found in the philosophical and legal foundations of the United States of America as presented in the Declaration of Independence and the Constitution, respectively. This book is an attempt to heal the social divide on abortion by starting with potential points of agreement. This may help facilitate the process of coming to a morally acceptable, politically feasible and commonsense resolution of the issue.

We believe one of the chief problems of the modern world to be the abandonment of the natural moral law as the basis of a rationally ordered human society, especially economic society. We have concurrence on this from such diverse authorities as Dr. Max Weismann, president of the Center for the Study of the Great Ideas in Chicago (co-founded by Dr. Weismann and Dr. Mortimer J. Adler, the late "Great Books" philosopher), Dr. Ahmed Subhy Mansour, president of the International Quranic Center in

---

[1] "Pro-Choice" is used in this book for reasons that will become clear as the argument develops.

- 1 -

Northern Virginia, and Dr. Norman G. Kurland, president of the Center for Economic and Social Justice ("CESJ") in Arlington, Virginia.

A dramatic illustration of how the natural law has been abandoned even by its ostensible defenders is what happened at the University of Notre Dame in South Bend, Indiana. We refer, of course, to the decision by the Trustees and President of the University to confer an honorary degree on President Barack Obama in 2009, apparently in defiance of a clear directive to the contrary issued by the American Catholic bishops.

We have no substantial objections to President Obama as a commencement speaker, at Notre Dame or anywhere else. We believe that there may have been, and probably were, better choices as speaker to embody what Notre Dame claims to represent. Nevertheless, the selection of a speaker, however controversial, is a matter of prudence. The objective good or evil of the invitation to President Obama is not a matter for human judgment.

We can, however, use what happened at Notre Dame to highlight the central problem of modern society: the near-total abandonment of the natural moral law as the basis of a just social order. Our leaders, even the most well-intentioned moral and political leaders, seem confused about the basis of society, even what it means to be human and a person. That being the case, what are the rest of us to do, especially when we look to our leaders for guidance?

Thus, we believe it is possible to take Mr. Obama's declaration that he desires to find a common ground between the Pro-life and the Pro-Choice positions not as a challenge, but as an invitation. If Mr. Obama is sincere in his desire to search for common ground on which to resolve the issue, this book might help start the process.

The point of this book, and the blog series on which it was based, is that there is a common ground between the Pro-Life movement and the Pro-Choice movement. This common ground is not, however, in the realm of moral philosophy (ethics). The common ground is in the realm of *politics*, "politics" being the art of the possible.

As the postings in the blog series tried to make clear, the common ground with the Pro-Choice movement is based on the right of choice claimed by the Pro-Choice movement. We assert that, given a right of choice, it applies equally to the Pro-Life movement. This conforms to principles of common sense as well as basic strategy. It does this by basing the argument on reason, and without humiliating the other side or compromising anyone's principles. As G. K. Chesterton explained in his book, *Saint Thomas Aquinas: "The Dumb Ox"*,

> It is no good to tell an atheist that he is an atheist; or to charge a denier of immortality with the infamy of denying it; or to imagine that one can force an opponent to admit he is wrong, by proving that he is wrong on somebody else's principles, but not on his own. After the great example of St. Thomas, the principle stands, or ought always to have stood established; that we must either not argue with a man at all, or we must argue on his grounds and not ours. We may do other things *instead* of arguing, according to our views of what is morally permissible, but if we argue we must argue "on the reasons and statements of the philosophers themselves."[2]

How do you do this? First, of course, you never box the other side in — especially by ranting that he is evil, a sinner, or anything else you think he might be. *Never*. As Sun Tzu pointed out in his *Art of War*,[3] you always leave the other side a way out. Demanding unconditional surrender is not a way out, nor does it allow the other side to save face. They will otherwise fight to the death — preferably yours. You *must* leave them a way out — just make

[2] G. K Chesterton, *Saint Thomas Aquinas: "The Dumb Ox."* New York: Doubleday Image Books, 1956, 95-96.
[3] Sun Tzu, *The Art of War, Translated and with an Introduction by Samuel B. Griffith*. New York: Oxford University Press, 1963.

sure that the way out is in the direction you want them to go. You then follow Miyamoto Musashi's teachings and leverage your opponent's strength against him.[4] His greatest strength then becomes his greatest weakness; the more he relies on his strength, the weaker he becomes.

Thus, by insisting that abortion is a right under free choice, Pro-Choice adherents have presented both sides with a common political ground and an opening — if choice as a right and a principle is followed consistently. No one can claim a right to choose and at the same time deny it to others. This is not only an essential starting point for dialogue between the two camps, it is also the rationale for and the basis of an economic agenda for the Pro-Life movement — and everyone else.

This book addresses the issue first by examining the foundation of the Pro-Life position: the natural law as the basis of a just social order. Part II then examines the natural law orientation of the U.S. Constitution. Both of these sections are lengthy (at least for this book), for many people are simply unaware of these arguments or their implications.

Part III builds on this by accepting — only for the sake of the argument and to get down to business — a right to choice. The point of Part III is, given that a right to choose is accepted in society (whether or not the right is regarded as just), that right must be applied equally to all, without discrimination — especially the right to choose *not* to do something.

Part IV outlines an approach to reforming and maintaining the institutions of society in a way that satisfies both the rights of individuals and the needs of society as a whole. This is called "social justice," a virtue the object of which is not the *particular* good of any individual or group, but the whole of the *common* good.

---

[4] Miyamoto Musashi, *The Book of Five Rings*. New York: Barnes and Noble, 1997.

Finally, Part V offers both sides a way to get what each claims they want: a decent life for everyone in a way that respects everyone's rights, without coercion or pressure from other individuals, groups, or the State itself.

This, then, is the true common ground, not only for Pro-Choice and Pro-Life, but for everyone: access to the means of acquiring and possessing private property in the means of production. This solves the problem of how to support human life economically in all phases of its development, before, during, and after birth: an economic agenda based on natural law principles and designed to support life from birth to natural death in a way that respects everyone's rights.

Being, as we noted, based on blog entries for the Short Attention Span 21st Century, all the chapters in this book are necessarily short. Further, the reader will notice that some of the sources used may not be considered truly scholarly, but popular. These are advantages. The most immediate need today is not an extended philosophical or legal treatment of the subject.

Instead, we need a brief, commonsense approach to a difficult problem. We need something to give guidelines that will allow people to use their native wit and intelligence within a framework of social justice that takes both our individual and social natures — that is, our political nature — into account. Once we look at the problem in the right way, we're more than halfway to a solution. We can finally get the economy and the whole of the social order off of artificial life support, and transform our institutions so that they naturally support life.

By implementing a private sector economic growth program along the lines of "Capital Homesteading,"[5] for example, every man, woman and child could receive the right to borrow, say, $7,000 per year of newly created, asset-backed money to purchase capital assets that pay for themselves out of future profits generated by the capital

---

[5] See Chapter 20.

itself. Given that the assumptions used in developing the Capital Homesteading proposal are valid, a child born today could accumulate nearly $500 thousand in tax-sheltered, income-generating capital assets by age 65. During that time, he or she would also potentially enjoy up to $46 thousand each year in after-tax dividend income, totaling approximately $1.6 million.[6]

The income generated by a "Capital Homestead" accumulation would have the potential to eliminate the current regressive payroll tax and solve the problem of the looming Social Security and Medicare deficit by gradually replacing State welfare entitlements — two-thirds of the federal budget! — with income from privately owned capital assets. Except for emergencies, consumer borrowing and thus the crushing burden of personal debt would be a thing of the past. Finally, increasing personal income by adding capital earnings to labor earnings and taxing all income at a single rate above a substantial and meaningful exemption (perhaps $100 thousand for a "typical" family of four) as "ordinary income," would rebuild the tax base. Government deficits could be eliminated and the mounting national debt repaid within a generation.

As should be obvious, the author is not a lawyer, a theologian, or a professional philosopher. Neither is CESJ a Catholic or even religious organization. This book is based on postings on "The Just Third Way" blog[7] from October 27, 2009 to November 19, 2009. Except for verifiable facts, everything is the writer's personal opinion as to the application of certain natural law principles of economic and social justice found in the binary economics of Louis Kelso and Mortimer Adler, and the social doctrine Pope Pius XI, respectively. Nothing in this book should be taken as asserting the official positions of the Center for Economic and Social Justice, the Catholic Church, or the Pro-Life movement.

---

[6] http://www.cesj.org/socialsecurity/projections-cha.htm.
[7] http://just3rdway.blogspot.com

Part I: The Law

1. The Political Animal

At the root of many of today's problems is a failure to understand our basic human nature as individuals and as social beings. This is a unique combination we call a "political animal."[1] We have lost our moral compass, our knowledge of the principles underlying what it means to be human. We no longer have the sense of a common ground on which we meet as mere members of the human race.

Nowhere is this more evident than with the issue of abortion. Society is divided on whether abortion is a fundamental human right, or so fundamentally wrong as to admit no question. Given that, whether or not they are justified by their faith in their beliefs, many people believe that there is a right to abortion on demand. Many others believe that no such right could possibly exist. The question then becomes what can be done to bring about a peaceful resolution to this problem.

At the heart of the problem is the issue of *personality* or *personhood*. There is a great deal of confusion about this relatively simple concept today. Part of the blame can be placed on the totalitarian movements that characterized the twentieth century. These were based on various forms of legal, moral, social, and even religious positivism that developed in Europe out of rejection of the Aristotelian/Thomist understanding of the natural moral law from the twelfth to the sixteenth centuries.[2] We see this re-

---

[1] "Man is by nature a political animal." Aristotle, *The Politics*, Book I.

[2] "Since the modern world began in the sixteenth century, nobody's system of philosophy has really corresponded to everybody's sense of reality; to what, if left to themselves, common men would call common sense. Each started with a paradox; a peculiar point of view demanding the sacrifice of what they

flected in the separation of *personhood* from *being* — the idea that a human *being* is not *necessarily* at the same time a human *person*.

The Nazis were adept at sowing this sort of confusion. The National Socialist Party of Germany took to the extreme the socialist tendency to redefine and eliminate natural rights whenever it became convenient or expedient to do so. Primary among the rights such totalitarians ignored or denied were, as we might expect, life and liberty (freedom of association), as well as the capacity of individual human beings to acquire and develop virtue — the "pursuit of happiness." By this means the Nazis undermined all that which defines us as human beings, and thus as human persons. Largely unnoticed among the rights the Nazis redefined away from being natural was the natural right to be an owner — the right *to* property. They then defined the exercise of property (the rights *of* property) in a way that made how an owner could use what he or she owned completely dependent on the will of the State.[3]

---

would call a sane point of view. . . A man had to believe something that no normal man would believe, if it were suddenly propounded to his simplicity; as that law is above right, or right is outside reason, or things are only as we think them, or everything is relative to a reality that is not there. The modern philosopher claims, like a sort of confidence man, that if once we will grant him this, the rest will be easy; he will straighten out the world, if once he is allowed to give this one twist to the mind." G. K. Chesterton, *Saint Thomas Aquinas: "The Dumb Ox."* New York: Doubleday Image Books, 1956, 145-146. See also the analysis in Dr. Heinrich Rommen, *The Natural Law.* Indianapolis, Indiana: Liberty Fund, Inc., 1998.

[3] "In its underlying theory Nazism denied the absolute character of property, and imposed obligations conditioning property tenure. Property without function was to be abolished. The acquisition of legal title was a continuous process, of which legitimate use was the essence. Ownership was not a right that stood by its own virtue, but a trusteeship for the discharge of the aims of the community. "All property is common property. The owner is

Nor is this restricted to the Nazis. Admittedly, closet socialists, when they are Christian — especially when they are Catholic — tend to deny (above all to themselves) that what they believe is in any way tainted with socialism. The Catholic Church, after all, has condemned socialism in no uncertain terms on many occasions. Such people forget (or ignore) the definition of socialism given by Karl Marx in *The Communist Manifesto* in 1848: "The theory of the communists can be summed up in the single sentence: abolition of private property."[4]

As any Thomist or Aristotelian can tell you, redefining something changes a thing's "substantial nature" — its essence. Redefining something makes the thing other than what it was. Redefinition thus abolishes the thing, even if you keep the same word or term for that which you have redefined. You have not changed the substantial nature of the thing that went before. You have merely given something else the same name, eliminating that which held the name previously.

Thus, all the concerned Christians, Jews, Muslims, and other adherents of religions with social teachings based on the natural law[5] who seek to circumvent the demands of the natural right *to* private property and the derived rights *of* private property by redefining what it means for something to be private property (whether they realize it or not) are socialists. This is because they thereby abolish private property for what it was, and turn it into what they want it to be. This is moral and legal positivism ("modernism" in "Catholic language") run amok.

---

obliged to administer it." Wunderlich, the National Socialist Conception of Landed Property, 12 Social Research 60 at 61, 66, 72 (1945), quoted in Howard R. Williams, *Cases and Materials on the Law of Property.* Brooklyn, New York: The Foundation Press, Inc., 1954, 47.
[4] Karl Marx and Friedrich Engels, *The Communist Manifesto.* London: Penguin Books, 1967, 96.
[5] See C. S. Lewis, *The Abolition of Man.* New York: Harper Collins, 2001.

To this we contrast the idea of *personalism*, the philosophy that places *persons* and personal relationships firmly grounded in the principles of the natural moral law at the center of theory and practice in science. "Science" includes the social sciences as well as the physical sciences. Personalism regards humanity, both as individuals and as members of groups, and respect for human dignity, as the focus of temporal activity. The perfection of human beings within a just social order in a manner consistent with nature is the "end" (in the philosophical sense) of that activity.

Personalism is an approach to Aristotelian/Thomist philosophy that emphasizes the natural rights of each human *being*, both individual and social. Personalism puts human *persons* at the center of all human activity. The natural right to private property (correctly defined) is an integral aspect of what it means for someone (or something) to be a "person," and thus have a social identity.

2. What is Man?

In the previous chapter we claimed that personality — personhood — and the natural right of private property (along with the full spectrum of other natural rights) are inextricably linked. These rights provide essential support for the dignity of each human person. Respect for individual natural rights is, in fact, an integral aspect of human dignity — *dignitas*.

Further, we found that private property is not the only natural right under assault these days. While abuses are frequent, most people recognize (at least to some extent) when the natural right of free association — liberty — is being attacked. There remains, however, a strong tendency to equivocate and downplay the implications of violations of our natural right to liberty. Further, our natural right to life may be universally recognized . . . but is subject to a multitude of positivist redefinitions that restrict it to select individuals and groups. This, as we might expect, is cause for serious concern.

Property, however, is just as important as life and liberty. This is because ownership of the means of production vests the owner with the means to sustain life for him- or herself and his or her dependents. Understand, of course, that "property" is not the thing owned. Property is the right to be an owner (the natural right *to* property), as well as the socially determined and defined rights *of* property — what an owner may do with what he or she possesses.

Property thereby empowers the owner with the means to resist unjust inroads on life and liberty by other individuals, groups, or even (or especially) the State itself. Life, liberty, and property are thus essential to empowering each individual with the ability to acquire and develop virtue: "pursue happiness." By acquiring and developing virtue an individual becomes more fully human and fitted for his or her proper end.

This is, in fact, why Pius XI and other popes condemned socialism. It is not because socialism seeks to abolish private property *per se*. Instead, socialism is condemned because the justification for abolishing private property results from an orientation and a philosophy that attacks and undermines the dignity of the human person. Socialism is based "on a theory of human society peculiar to itself and irreconcilable with true Christianity. Religious socialism, Christian socialism, are contradictory terms; no one can be at the same time a good Catholic and a true socialist."[1]

Note that citing a moral authority that also happens to be a religious figure implies neither an endorsement of nor a reliance on religious revelation for the argument; it is used to illustrate and support, not prove. Catholicism shares a common social (as opposed to religious or revelatory) basis in the natural moral law with all the major religions. In addition, the natural moral law — which we will examine presently — provides the basis for all three of humanity's discrete societies: civil (the State), domestic (the family), or religious (temple, church, mosque, synagogue, *etc.*).

The capacity to acquire and develop that virtue (the habit of doing good) that makes up the natural moral law is what defines us as human. The natural moral law, regardless of the religious significance or authority (or lack thereof) of the teacher, cannot be rejected as the basis for a sane society. This is true regardless of our private feelings about the validity of religious revelation or the institution of private property.

The abolition of private property, an important right embodied in the natural moral law, is simply the most obvious and the surest indication that a proposal is social-

---

[1] Pope Pius XI, *Quadragesimo Anno* ("On the Restructuring of the Social Order"), 1931, § 120.

ist. It thereby constitutes an attack on essential human dignity and the natural moral law. You can have a socialism that permits private ownership, but does not recognize that ownership as a natural right. In moral philosophy it is the failure to recognize private ownership of the means of production as a natural right that is the basic problem with socialism, not the fact of private ownership or lack thereof. The former is an ethical problem, the latter an economic problem, albeit an extremely serious one.

The rights to life, liberty, and property however, have been under continual assault since the sixteenth century. There was at that time the rebirth of an idea rooted in one of the very few mistakes Aristotle made. This was an error that Aquinas went to great lengths to correct.

Not coincidentally, this error experienced its renaissance at the same time that the basis of the natural law shifted from Nature (that is, Intellect or reason) to Will — that is, personal faith in something that a believer accepts as a revelation of the truth. The shift from Intellect to Will as the basis of the law is, as the great Aristotelian philosopher Mortimer Adler pointed out, one of the most significant sources for the establishment and maintenance of the totalitarian State.

Aristotle's error was to conclude that not all human beings have the same ("analogously complete") capacity to acquire and develop virtue. Thus, most people would lack the full ability to conform themselves to the dictates of the natural moral law. Instead (according to Aristotle), each individual has a different capacity to acquire and develop different kinds of virtue. Some creatures, "human only in appearance," do not have any capacity to acquire and develop virtue at all. Aristotle called these creatures that are human only in appearance, "natural slaves." Natural slaves require others to take care of them, whether the caretaker is another individual who is a full or partial human, or (as is the case with barbarian nations) the State itself.

The bottom line to Aristotle's thought — and the reason Aquinas worked so hard to correct the problem — is that, carrying this line of reasoning to its logical conclusion, some people end up being considered less human than others. Still others are thought of as not human at all. Full, even "partial" humanity becomes conditional on something other than mere existence, that is, something other than *being*.

If someone is strong enough to force acceptance of the case that certain individuals or even types or classes of people are not human or are not fully human, you can do anything to them that you want. This is because, not being human, they do not have human rights based on the natural moral law. They are subject to control or elimination at the will or whim of the majority, or can be imprisoned or put to death at the whim of the ruler or the will of the majority. These can include the unborn, the crippled, the mentally deficient, those who believe in the wrong religion or no religion, those with unacceptable political ideas, are social misfits, have the wrong sexual orientation, *etc., etc.* — anyone, in short, against whom we have a grudge, or who annoys us in some way.

3. What is a Person?

In the previous chapter we looked briefly at Aristotle's error in asserting that people all have different capacities to acquire and develop virtue. We then examined some of the conclusions that necessarily follow the belief that some people are less human than others, while still others are not human at all.

Being less human (or not human) means that someone does not have the full spectrum of natural rights (or any rights at all) that necessarily accompany the human condition. This is logical, for if you are not a full human *being* (that is, you do not exist completely as a human), how could you possibly be a full human *person*? If you are not human, of course you cannot have human rights, and are, therefore, not a person.

This is because only "persons" have rights, and only human beings can be human persons. A "person" is that which has rights, while a "thing" is the object of a right. A person, *e.g.*, owns, while a thing is owned. That which has the full spectrum of rights is a full person, while anything with less than the full spectrum of rights is either not a full person, or not a person at all.

Aristotle's concept of partial humanity raises the question as to whether it is possible to be a human *being*, and yet not a human *person*. This is where a philosophy of natural law comes into play. If the law — and thus rights — is based on Nature (that is, what the human race has decided in all times and places constitutes the "good" as reflected from some absolute source), then the law is "built in" to each and every member of the human race.

Consequently, each and every human being has by his or her own nature, that is, by *being* itself, possession of the full spectrum of natural rights inherent in the mere fact of existence. That is, if we base the natural law on

what we discern of human nature as a reflection of absolute good, the fact that someone is defined as a human
being automatically means that someone is also a human
person. With respect to humanity, *being* and *personality*
(personhood) are inseparable. Natural rights are inalienable, including life, liberty, property, and the pursuit of
happiness.

If, however, we base the natural law on something
other than what we can discern of the absolute good, then
the concept of inalienable rights is abolished. This is the
case when we base the law on some religious revelation
or, worse, reject the idea of natural law altogether and
base human positive law on the "general will" or something else. Everything, as Heinrich Rommen noted in *The
Natural Law*,[1] then becomes subject to change. This
clears the way for pure moral relativism, even nihilism.

By abandoning the idea of natural law based on absolute good and discerned by reason, we open the door to
such moral and legal sophistries as partial- or non-
personhood of that which is clearly human. We find in our
understanding of the natural law why this sort of thing is
both appalling logic and bad law.

A short time ago as of this writing the *Wall Street
Journal* ran an article extolling Professor Michael Sandel's course on justice at Harvard. The article related how
its popularity and Dr. Sandel's unique approach to the
subject presumably indicated a return to the premier
temporal virtue of justice as the basis of the social order.[2]
This appeared to be telling us something. As we noted in
a letter to the *Wall Street Journal* (not published) and as
Dr. Norman Kurland, president of CESJ, has been saying
for years, there is a great hunger for justice in the world
— and that means for a sound understanding of the natural moral law. This is a hunger that is not being met ei-

---

[1] Heinrich Rommen, *The Natural Law*. Indianapolis, Indiana:
Liberty Fund, Inc., 1998, 51-52.
[2] Charlotte Allen, "Justice for All: A Class in Ethical Sudoku,"
The Wall Street Journal, 10/09/09, W13.

ther by State imposition of desired results, or private sector efforts to maintain an unsustainable *status quo.*

Unfortunately, Dr. Sandel did not appear to be teaching *justice.* As we noted in our letter to the editor, the fact that approximately a thousand students sign up for Professor Sandel's class argues a great hunger for justice, just as Dr. Kurland has been saying. The problem with the class, however, is that (as described in the article) it didn't seem to be about *justice.* "Justice," according to Aristotle and Aquinas, is the habit a person has of rendering to others what is due to them.

Instead, Professor Sandel's students were getting situations based in utilitarianism that only by a long and extremely tortuous stretch of the imagination could come under *prudence,* not *justice.* Acts of prudence, of course, assume a solid grounding in justice, the premier natural virtue, something the students didn't appear to be getting from Professor Sandel. The largely contrived ethical dilemmas with which the students were confronted — variations on the "lifeboat scenario" so popular among relativists — failed to take into account the fact that, as far as "value" is concerned, each innocent human life is, in justice, of equal value. Even a single innocent individual may not, in justice, be sacrificed for the good of the many.

In our letter we suggested that Professor Sandel consider reorienting his class to conform to the ideas in the "Great Books of the Western World" program pioneered by Dr. Mortimer Adler and Dr. Robert Hutchins of the University of Chicago. As a good source for Professor Sandel, his students, and anyone else interested in the natural law basis of western civilization, we directed him to the Center for the Study of the Great Ideas in Chicago,[3] co-founded by Dr. Adler and Max Weismann. Although we copied Dr. Sandel on the letter, we received no reply.

Naturally, we weren't going to waste a great letter like that on one person, so we copied a number of people, in-

---

[3] www.thegreatideas.org

cluding Dr. Max Weismann, president of the Center for the Study of the Great Ideas in Chicago. Even though Dr. Weismann as of this writing has more immediate irons in the fire that demand his attention, he sent us two articles by Dr. Mortimer J. Adler on justice and the natural law, which were, in part, the inspiration for the blog postings that were the basis for this book.

Dr. Adler, of course, was not only America's premier Aristotelian philosopher of the 20th century and the co-founder with Robert Maynard Hutchins of the Great Books of the Western World program at the University of Chicago. Dr. Adler was also co-founder with Dr. Weismann of the Center for the Study of the Great Ideas, and co-author with Louis O. Kelso of the mis-titled yet profound *The Capitalist Manifesto* (1958), and the equally mis-titled yet revolutionary monograph, *The New Capitalists* (1961). These are the books that laid the groundwork for binary economics.

Why do we call *The New Capitalists* "revolutionary" when we characterize *The Capitalist Manifesto* as "merely" profound? Because *The New Capitalists* calls into question the most fundamental assumption of modern economics. This is an assumption that keeps the great mass of people tied to the wage system and utterly dependent on the wealthy elite or the State through the monopoly on money creation and access to existing accumulations of savings — and thus subject to redefinitions of natural rights and even of humanity itself. Kelso and Adler make this clear in the subtitle of *The New Capitalists*: "A Proposal to Free Economic Growth from the Slavery of Savings."

Both of Kelso and Adler's books and the whole of binary economics are, as we might expect, solidly grounded in natural law theory. This raises the question as to what, exactly, is this thing we call the "natural law"?

4. What is Natural Law?

In the previous chapter we noted that Dr. Max Weismann had sent us two articles by Dr. Mortimer J. Adler on the natural law and justice. With Father William J. Ferree, S.M., Ph.D.,[1] Dr. Adler might be considered one of the great philosophers of the Just Third Way.

One thing on which we've insisted for some time, as the "Keynote Address"[2] we gave at the centenary of the Central Bureau of the Catholic Central Union of America in 2008 makes clear, is that the restructuring of the social (and economic) order must be in conformity with the natural moral law. Not unnaturally, this raises the question as to what, exactly, is the natural law.

As Dr. Adler explained, "Let us first be clear that by 'natural law' we mean principles of human conduct, not the laws of nature discovered by the physical sciences." That is, the natural law is the way human beings are supposed to act in accordance with their own human nature. It is not the set of mechanical rules that govern how the universe physically operates. "The idea of a natural right order to which all things, including human beings, should conform is one of the most ancient and universal notions." Dr. Adler completed this thought by observing,

> In Western society, especially from the Roman jurists and the theologians of the Middle Age[s] on, we find the doctrine of the natural moral law for man. It is the source of moral standards, the basis of moral judgments, and the measure of justice in the man-

---

[1] Rev. William J. Ferree. S.M., Ph.D., *The Act of Social Justice*. Washington, DC: The Catholic University of America Press, 1943; *Introduction to Social Justice*. Arlington, Virginia: Center for Economic and Social Justice, 1997.

[2] http://www.cesj.org/thirdway/ccua-keynote-08-0809.htm.

made laws of the State. If the law of the State runs counter to the precepts of the natural law, it is held to be unjust.[3]

Thus, "the first precept of natural law is to seek the good and avoid evil." As a basic principle, however, this is nice, but nebulous until and unless it can be applied in everyday life. "Such a general principle is useless for organized society unless we can use it to specify various types of rights and wrongs. That is precisely what man-made, or positive, law tries to do." Dr. Adler continued,

Thus, the natural law tells us only that stealing is wrong because it inflicts injury, but the positive law of larceny defines the various kinds and degrees of theft and prescribes the punishments therefor.[4]

For anyone already familiar with the principles underlying CESJ's Just Third Way, this is one of those "stop me if you've heard this" moments, or (as Yogi Berra would say) *déjà vu* all over again. Dr. Heinrich Rommen said virtually the same thing in *his* book on the natural law:

"Thou shalt not steal" presupposes the institution of private property as pertaining to the natural law; but not, for example, the feudal property arrangements of the Middle Ages or the modern capitalist system. Since the natural law lays down general norms only, it is the function of the positive law to undertake the concrete, detailed regulation of real and personal property and to prescribe the formalities for conveyance of ownership.[5]

Human positive law is not set in stone. As both Aristotle and Aquinas observed, "particular rules of laws should [not] be the same in different times, places, and conditions." The basic precepts of the natural law are discernible by the use of human reason. Dr. Adler did not

---

[3] www.cooperativeindividualism.org/adler_naturallaw.html.
[4] *Ibid.*
[5] Rommen, *The Natural Law, op. cit.*, 59.

cite Aquinas on this, but in the treatise on law in the *Summa*, "the Angelic Doctor" stated quite clearly that law is found in reason alone.[6]

Reflecting on Dr. Adler's explanation, we conclude that it is humanity's task as "political animals" to tailor our institutions, among which are positive laws, as well as customs and traditions, to conform as closely as possible to the essential principle of the natural law: good is to be done, evil avoided. Of course, we have to take into consideration the constraints imposed by the existing culture and institutions, human wants and needs, the physical environment, and so on. This is how Father William Ferree defined the "common good": the network of institutions (social structures) within which human beings as political animals carry out their business of living. The chief business of life is to acquire and develop virtue, thereby becoming more fully human by conforming ourselves ever more closely to our own nature.

Dr. Adler did not go as far as that, but Pope Pius XI developed the idea of a specific ("particular") "act of social justice" that is directed specifically at the reform of the institutions of the common good. (There is an explanation in *Introduction to Social Justice* why traditional philosophers like Dr. Adler do not — yet — accept the idea of "social justice" as a "particular virtue," but that does not concern us for the purposes of this discussion.) The bottom line is that we are not helpless in the face of badly structured institutions or poorly organized societies. It is within our power, as members of organized groups, to effect beneficial social change directly on our institutional environment.

As we might expect, not everyone agrees with this view of the natural law. For thousands of years there has been a school of thought called "positivism" that holds that human positive law is purely a matter of agreement among people joined together in society, a convention not

---

[6] Ia IIae q. 90 a. 1

rooted in our very identity as human beings. That being the case, you can pretty much do anything you like as long as you can get enough people to go along with it. Dr. Adler referred to this belief as "conventionalism" and "positivism."

5. Positivism and its Dangers

As we saw in the previous chapter, not everyone agrees that human positive law is or even needs to be a reflection of an eternally valid natural law. For thousands of years some people have held that positive law is purely a matter of convention, of agreement among peoples. If you can get enough people to agree with you on what the law — and thus morality — is, then you can do it. Mortimer J. Adler called this belief "conventionalism" and "positivism." Heinrich Rommen called it simply "positivism," while Pope St. Pius X and Pope Pius XI employed the somewhat confusing theological term, "modernism."[1]

Dr. Adler then explained that, while Christians are the largest group of thinkers who base the natural law on what reason discerns and discovers of human nature, this particular orientation is not confined to Christians. We find it (as we might expect) in Aristotle, Cicero, even modern secularists such as Kant and Hegel, as well as in Jews who follow the philosophy of Moses Maimonides and Muslims who follow that of Ibn Khaldûn. The essential point of agreement is that there is somewhere a source of absolute truth. People can disagree, sometimes violently, on what to call this source — most people call it "God" or some variation thereon — but all agree that there is defi-

---

[1] What the Catholic Church calls "modernism" really doesn't have anything to do with being modern, but is a weird grab-bag of philosophies and theological thought discredited centuries, sometimes millennia ago, and periodically resurrected and given an attractive new name until people catch on. Similarly, "liberalism" in "Catholic language" doesn't mean political or social liberalism, but a specific religious belief that all religions are really the same. "Liberalism" is the theory that, *e.g.*, a Satanist, a Hindu, and a Southern Baptist all have the same religious beliefs, and any differences are merely semantic.

nitely something there, and that this source is "good." Consequently, such things as theft, murder, adultery, false witness, and so on, are contrary to nature.

Unfortunately, what happens is that some people (especially devout religious believers and, paradoxically, militant secularists and atheists) have the tendency to claim that the natural moral law is not truly an aspect of human nature, but of divine command. We do not discover the natural law by observing what the human race in all times and places has decided is "good." Instead, the law is contained in some revelation by some deity, whether something actually worshipped as a god or goddess, or the State that has made itself into a god.

In the Middle Ages, this resulted in an intellectual "war" between the philosophers who believed that "law is found in reason alone,"[2] and those who believed that the law is revealed directly to man by God. That is, there was a conflict between the philosophers who held that the natural law can be figured out by anybody with a brain through the process of reason, and those who believed that the natural law is found in whatever a believer believes to be an expression of the will of a deity, e.g., the Bible, the Torah, the Quran, and so on — that is, in the positive expression of God's Will found in a document believed to be of divine origin.

Obviously, there are some problems inherent in the two approaches, one of which bases things on reason and the other on faith — or there wouldn't be a conflict. Oddly enough, however, the only problem (although it is significant) with the "reason alone" people is that when they tend to accept materialism they also tend to reject anything relating to ethics — moral philosophy — as faith-based. Morality so-defined thus has no place in civil society. This actually goes against their own principles, but it's enough to insert a great deal of confusion into modern society. The bottom line is that anything labeled "moral-

---

[2] *Ibid.*

ity" becomes, *ipso facto*, "religion," and must be actively suppressed.

Unfortunately, faith-based people tend to overreact. They make two mistakes to the materialists' one. One, when the dictates of reason seem to be in contradiction to their interpretation of revelation, there is a strong tendency to claim that reason *must* be in error *because* it contradicts their personal faith. Two (and much more serious), people who base the law on faith have a very, very strong tendency to try and force their specific religious beliefs and practices on others. Inevitably they seek to use the coercive power of the State to enforce their demands.

In reaction, the materialists reinforce their claim that anything based on the natural law — moral philosophy (ethics) — is "religion" and must, therefore, never be imposed by force. This is a half-truth that starts the cycle all over again. The only results are an intensification of the conflict, increasing levels of frustration, prejudice, and bigotry on both sides. Widespread confusion about the nature of the human person and of society itself then leads to more confusion. The materialists and the religion-based individuals and groups both end up supporting their positions on the basis of faith, not of reason.

The basic issue remains unaddressed. If the natural law is found in reason alone, as Aquinas maintained, it applies to everybody. No one is exempted from the obligation to acquire and develop virtue and thereby become more fully human. If, however, the natural law is found only in some revelation — even the revelation of "science" — then only believers in that revelation can become more fully human. By logical development of this belief, it becomes imperative that whoever believes in the divine origin of a specific revelation force it on others for the others' own good, whether you call it faith or reason.

6. Reason or Will?

In the previous chapter, we discovered that materialists who reject faith, and believers who reject reason, are in reality making the same mistake, only from different directions. Both tend to view the world in terms of faith *or* reason (or, more accurately, demonize something the other side calls "science" or "religion"), not faith *and* reason.

Thus, if you believe that the Bible, the Torah, the Quran, or the writings of the gods of secular academia contain specific instructions for the conduct of human life, you tend to reject the underlying principle(s) in favor of specific applications that may or may not be valid in a particular case.[1] The urge is to take your own opinion as to the meaning of some revelation, whether religious or scientific, and try to force it on everyone else.

The other approach is to look on such authorities as expressing general principles of truth as those principles apply within a particular sphere. The problem then becomes discerning the real basis for the natural law, and going from there, rather than using coercion to force others to go along with your private interpretation.

This is the whole point of the analysis in Dr. Heinrich Rommen's book, *The Natural Law*, written in the wake of the Nazi tyranny in an effort to explain the origins of totalitarianism. Dr. Rommen, a student of Father Heinrich Pesch, S.J., the great solidarist philosopher, was a member of the *Königswinterkreis*. This "King's Winter Circle"

---

[1] See Michael D. Greaney, *Social Justice Betrayed*. St. Louis, Missouri: Central Bureau, Catholic Central Union of America, 2000; republished with changes in, *In Defense of Human Dignity, Essays on the Just Third Way: A Natural Law Perspective*. Arlington, Virginia: Economic Justice Media, 2008, 1-103.

study group was headed by Father Oswald von Nel Bru-
ening, S.J., who drafted *Quadragesimo Anno* ("On the Restructuring of the Social Order"), 1931, under the direction of Pope Pius XI.

One of Germany's leading jurists, Dr. Rommen was
forced to flee Germany in the 1930s. He ended up teaching at Georgetown University, although (oddly) not at the
law school. As Rommen explained the position of those
who rely on faith rather than reason in matters of science
(and, yes, theology and philosophy are sciences),

> For Duns Scotus morality depends on the will of God.
> A thing is good not because it corresponds to the na-
> ture of God or, analogically, to the nature of man, but
> because God so wills. Hence the *lex naturalis* could be
> other than it is even materially or as to content, be-
> cause it has no intrinsic connection with God's es-
> sence, which is self-conscious in His intellect. For Sco-
> tus, therefore, the laws of the second table of the De-
> calogue were no longer unalterable. . . . Now . . . an
> evolution set in which, in the doctrine of William of
> Occam (d. *cir.* 1349) on the natural moral law, would
> lead to pure moral positivism, indeed to nihilism.[2]

This, then, appears to be the major philosophical issue
of our day: whether the natural moral law (and thus the
positive law) is to be based on Nature (Intellect/Reason),
that is, on what we can discern of divine Nature reflected
in human nature . . . or whether the natural moral law is
purely a matter of opinion, and whoever is the strongest
makes and enforces positive law based on whatever he or
she can get away with. As Mortimer Adler observed,

> The denial of natural rights, the natural moral law,
> and natural justice leads not only to the positivist
> conclusion that man-made law alone determines what
> is just and unjust. It also leads to a corollary which
> inexorably attaches itself to that conclusion — that

---

[2] Rommen, *The Natural Law, op. cit.*, 51-52.

might makes right. This is the very essence of absolute or despotic government.[3]

So, to answer the question with which we began this discussion on the natural law and reiterate and restate Mortimer Adler's definition, the natural law is the body of principles that guide human conduct. These principles, discernible completely through the use of human reason, are based on understanding of our own nature as we see it manifested in the behavior of our fellow man and our beliefs as to what constitutes the "good" measured against what people have in all times and places agreed is "good."

---

[3] Mortimer Adler, "The Meaning of Natural Law"
http://radicalacademy.com/adlernaturallaw.htm.

Part II: The Constitution

7. A Question of Being

In *Roe v. Wade*,[1] the justices of the Supreme Court of the United States declared that they did not know whether a fetus is a human being, but that "it" is not a person as that term is used in the Constitution. As the Wikipedia explains (admittedly not a recognized legal authority),

> In **Section IX** [of the Court's opinion], the Court added that there was no legal grounds for factoring into this balancing test any right to life of the unborn fetus. The fetus would have such a right if it were defined as a legal person for purposes of the Fourteenth Amendment, but the original intent of the Constitution (up to the enactment of the Fourteenth Amendment in 1868) did not include protection of the unborn. The Court emphasized that its determination of whether a fetus can enjoy constitutional protection neither meant to reference, nor intervene in, the question of when life begins: "We need not resolve the difficult question of when life begins. When those trained in the respective disciplines of medicine, philosophy, and theology are unable to arrive at any consensus, the judiciary, at this point in the development of man's knowledge, is not in a position to speculate as to the answer."[2]

The logical flaw in this line of reasoning is immediately apparent to anyone with a natural law orientation. The United States is founded on the belief that "all men are created equal and are endowed by their Creator with certain unalienable rights." As should be unnecessary to

---

[1] 410 U.S. 113 (1973)
[2] http://en.wikipedia.org/wiki/Roe_v._Wade

state (which means it *is* necessary), the term "men" includes not only adult males, but females as well as anything else defined as "human," at any stage or condition of physical, mental, or spiritual development.

This is easy to understand. Whether someone is *actually* or *potentially* fully human is irrelevant. "Actuality" and "potentiality" are both stages of "being." In Aristotelian/Thomist philosophy (the basis of western civilization), a thing cannot both "be" and "not be." This is called the "law of contradiction." The law of contradiction is a basic principle of logic and philosophy. Consequently, everything that is, is, while everything that is not, is not.

This sounds confusing, but reflect on it for a moment. If something "is," it is fully what it is, without qualification. A thing cannot partially exist, or only be a part of what it is. It either exists, or it does not exist. Period. A 98-pound weakling is only potentially a Charles Atlas with the power to return sand to a bully's face and take back the girl — but the weakling (if we believe comic book ads) does have the potential to become a Charles Atlas. Both the weakling and Mr. Atlas — as well as the bully and the girl — are fully human. All have the same potential to have rippling muscles and sand-kicking capability as anyone else. Both exist as fully as the others exist.

Similarly, a fetus has the potential to actualize as a fully developed human being. There is no question that a fetus is as fully human as, say, Barack Obama. "Potential" humans and "actual" humans are both human in the same sense of the term because both "are" as fully as the other. Consequently, both a fetus and Barack Obama each participate in "being" as fully as does the other. Both are thus full human beings. Within the natural law framework that provides and justifies the basis of the United States, both are therefore "persons."

The argument of the American Founding Fathers was that "the present King of Great Britain" violated their natural rights to life, liberty, property, and pursuit of happiness.[3] That is, the Founding Fathers claimed that rights ultimately come not from the State, that is, the king, but from "the laws of nature and of nature's God." According to the Founding Fathers, possession of natural rights is contingent only on mere existence. To impose any other requirement denies not only the political philosophy used to justify separation from Great Britain, but renders the American Revolution an unjustified act of rebellion.

In *Roe v. Wade*, however, the Supreme Court effectively declared that possession of natural rights — personhood or personality — depends not upon mere existence of the human fetus. Existence is an obvious fact, although the majority opinion denied its implications. Instead, possession of natural rights was made contingent on "original intent" of the framers of the 14th Amendment, as well as the "viability" of the fetus.

The 14th Amendment, however, enacted in 1868, was intended to extend the rights of citizenship to *all* Americans, and the protection of the law to *all* people. In relevant part, the Amendment states,

No State shall make or enforce any law which shall abridge the privileges or immunities of citizens of the United States; nor shall any State deprive any person of life, liberty, or property, without due process of law; nor deny to any person within its jurisdiction the equal protection of the laws.

---

[3] Because of the slavery issue, property was not mentioned in the Declaration of Independence. Property does, however, figure prominently in the Virginia Declaration of Rights that provided the template and model for the Declaration of Independence.

8. Personality

The original intent of the framers of the 14th Amendment of the Constitution of the United States was to extend the status of "person" to human beings who had, as a necessary precondition of involuntary servitude, been denied personality or personhood. Before the Emancipation Proclamation of 1863 and the 13th Amendment of the Constitution (1865), black slaves had not been construed as "persons," but as "property," that is, "things." They could thus be owned, and disposed of as their owners desired, just as the traditional rights of private property declared.

To correct this serious deficiency, over which a war had just been fought that cost the lives of an estimated 618,000 soldiers on both sides[1] the framers of the 14th Amendment went to great lengths to try and ensure that no human being at whatever stage of physical or social development or of previous condition of servitude could ever again be redefined as a "non-person" and thereby removed from the full and equal protection of the law.

The key word in the 14th Amendment is "person." The Supreme Court of the United States explicitly acknowledged this in its opinion in *Roe v. Wade*. From there, however, the argument degenerated. If, as the Supreme Court argued, the original intent of the framers of the 14th Amendment omitted unborn human beings from the category of "person," then equal protection of life, liberty, and property does not apply to human fetuses. This reasoning is flawed on three counts.

One (as we noted in the previous chapter), the Court's reasoning made personality — personhood — contingent upon something other than mere existence as a human

---

[1] http://www.civilwarhome.com/casualties.htm

being at any stage of development or condition of life. This abrogated the natural law justification for the existence of the United States as set forth in the Declaration of Independence, and undermined the authority of the Supreme Court itself.

Two, the "original intent" argument does not hold up. The framers of the 14th Amendment clearly sought to extend equal protection of the law to human beings who had previously been denied the status of person. In an astounding example of legal sophistry and mental gymnastics, the Supreme Court used the 14th Amendment in *Roe v. Wade* to deny the status of person to unborn human beings and restrict equal protection under the law only to those whom the Court deemed worthy of such protection.

Three, the Supreme Court claimed because the framers of the 14th Amendment did not specifically mention the fetus, and clearly did not have the fetus in mind (true — why should they?), the fetus is therefore not a person as that term is used in the Constitution. This argument ignored the 9th and 10th Amendments.

The 9th Amendment is that, "The enumeration in the Constitution, of certain rights, shall not be construed to deny or disparage others retained by the people." The 10th Amendment is that, "The powers not delegated to the United States by the Constitution, nor prohibited by it to the States, are reserved to the States respectively, or to the people."

9. States' Rights

In the previous chapter we noted that the 9th Amendment to the U.S. Constitution is, "The enumeration in the Constitution, of certain rights, shall not be construed to deny or disparage others retained by the people." The 10th Amendment is, "The powers not delegated to the United States by the Constitution, nor prohibited by it to the States, are reserved to the States respectively, or to the people."

In *Roe v. Wade*, the U.S. Supreme Court claimed because the fetus is not mentioned in the 14th Amendment, and because the framers of the 14th Amendment clearly did not have the fetus in mind when they drafted it, the fetus is not a person as that term is used in the 14th Amendment. This is very bad Constitutional law, especially in light of the 9th and 10th Amendments, to say nothing of the Declaration of Independence (the document which, while not itself law, gives context to the Constitution), all of which must be referenced if we are to understand the 14th Amendment and its alleged applicability in taking away the natural rights of the fetus.

Of the two, by far the most relevant in interpreting the 14th Amendment is the 9th Amendment. To argue that the fetus has no rights because the 14th Amendment does not mention the fetus, or because the framers of the 14th Amendment did not have the fetus in mind when they wrote it, directly contradicts the 9th Amendment.

Constitutionally and consistently, the Supreme Court would have to argue that, because of the 9th Amendment, the mere fact that the fetus is not mentioned in the 14th Amendment means that the fetus must be presumed to be a human being and thus a person until and unless it can be proved otherwise. This, the Court explicitly stated, it was not prepared to do. The Court's decision thereby contradicts the principle in the 9th Amendment that enumerating specific rights is not to be taken as denying any rights not so specified.

We would otherwise have to conclude that the intent of the framers of the 14th Amendment was to *revoke* the 9th Amendment, and make possession of all rights (and thus personhood) dependent on the will of the State. This is clearly not the case, nor did the Supreme Court attempt to make that argument. The justices simply ignored the 9th and 10th Amendments in their decision. Under the 10th Amendment, of course, it is perfectly proper for any state to prohibit abortion, because a presumed right to an abortion is not *specifically* mentioned in the Constitution.

Thus, the Supreme Court contradicted itself. First, the Court argued that the fetus does not retain the natural right to life. This is because the fetus is not specifically mentioned in the 14th Amendment. This interpretation violates the 9th Amendment, because the 9th Amendment protects all rights not specifically mentioned otherwise in the Constitution.

The Court then maintained that the federal government in the person of the Supreme Court can overturn any and all state laws prohibiting or limiting abortion. This violates the 10th Amendment because the power to legalize abortion is not specifically mentioned anywhere in the Constitution as being vested in the federal government. The Court thereby figured out a way to have its cake and eat it, too, by the simple expedient of doing exactly the opposite of what the Constitution allows the Court to do.

10. Personal Sovereignty

In the previous chapter we discovered that the Supreme Court of the United States appeared to have contradicted itself in the decision it rendered in *Roe v. Wade*. Further, the basis for the decision seems to have been in conflict with the philosophy of government espoused by the Founding Fathers of the American Republic.

The problem, of course, is obvious. The justices in *Roe v. Wade* took a substantially different view of the Constitution than did the framers of the Constitution and the authors of the 14th Amendment, even as they cited original intent. As far as the Founding Fathers of the United States were concerned, all rights come from individual people organized as a political entity. The Constitution, consistent with the political philosophy embodied in Thomism and Roman law, is a revocable grant of rights from the people to the federal government. That is, rights are presumed to flow from the people to the State. Thus, under true "original intent," the presumption must be that the fetus has a natural right to life, which right overrides any derived or statutory right a woman — or man — might have to choose abortion.

The Supreme Court in *Roe v. Wade* clearly took a different view of sovereignty: that rights flow from the State to the people; that the State, not people, is the ultimate sovereign. Under this orientation, people have only those rights that the State has decided to grant them. Everyone and everything becomes, ironically as expressed by the United States Supreme Court itself in *Pierce v. Society of Sisters*,[1] "a mere creature of the State."

This is a complete reversal of the political philosophy on which the United States was founded. It is also a flat

---

[1] 268 U.S. 510 (1925).

contradiction of essential precepts of moral philosophy. As Pope Pius XI expressed it, "Only man, the human person, and not society in any form is endowed with reason and a morally free will."[2] That is, only the human person, not human creations including any and all forms of society (even the State and the U.S. Supreme Court) has the morally free will and the correlative capacity to acquire and develop virtue — "pursue happiness" — and thus the natural rights that necessarily accompany the human condition.

Parallels between the Court's reasoning in *Roe v. Wade* and that of the German judiciary under the Third Reich are almost too obvious even to mention. The short but influential pamphlet Binding and Hoche published in 1920, *Permission to Destroy Life Unworthy of Life (Die Freigabe der Vernichtung Lebensunwerten Lebens)* comes forcibly to mind.[3] Further, if we accept the Court's reasoning, then the 14th Amendment does not include homosexuals, Jews, communists, and a host of other possibly unpopular or presumably socially dangerous groups in the definition of "person." After all, the framers did not mention such individuals or groups specifically in the Amendment, and clearly did not have them in mind when framing the Amendment. A strong case can be and has, in fact, been made that equal protection of the law does not extend to such mental, social, or physical defectives: "the unfit."

Even Irving Fisher, the man declared by Nobel Laureate Milton Friedman to be "America's greatest economist," published a tract in 1909 on the advisability of instituting a program of "national hygiene," including forced sterilization of physical and mental defectives and other measures eventually adopted by the Nazis.[4] Using the ration-

---

[2] *Divini Redemptoris*, § 29.

[3] http://en.wikipedia.org/wiki/Life_unworthy_of_life

[4] Irving Fisher, "National Vitality, Its Wastes and Conservation." Vol. 3 of the Report of the National Conservation Commission issued in 1909 as Senate document no. 676, 60th Congress, 2d Session.

ale of the United States Supreme Court in *Roe v. Wade*, it would be a relatively simple matter to do what the German judiciary did under the Third Reich and redefine anyone categorized as social, mental, physical, or economic undesirables as non-persons, and dispose of them.

11. The Role of the State

Some people have argued that opposition to abortion is purely a religious issue. The State, therefore, can make no laws prohibiting abortion or limiting it any way. If opposition to abortion is, in fact, purely a religious issue, that would indeed be the case. At no level, whether local, state, or federal, could any form or branch of government make any law restricting or prohibiting abortion. We are ignoring for the sake of the argument that the State does, in fact, have the power to make laws restricting or prohibiting religious practices if they cause harm to individuals, groups, or the common good as a whole. This was the justification for outlawing plural marriage as practiced among some branches of the Church of Jesus Christ of Latter Day Saints — "the Mormons."

The point, however, is that if opposition to abortion is a purely religious issue, then support for abortion cannot be purely a civil issue. As a matter of consistency and of common sense, if opposition to abortion is a religious issue, then support for abortion is also a religious issue. Any form of support for abortion by government at any level would necessarily be a violation of the 1st Amendment as it would, in effect, establish a State religion.

No, the only rational approach to the abortion issue is on the basis of civil rights. Why someone opposes or supports abortion is irrelevant, whether that someone is a convinced deist who thinks that God has commanded women to have abortions at will, or a devout atheist who believes that the State has no right to make politically motivated decisions as to who and what constitutes a "person." That being the case, the issue must be handled in the public arena, with both sides accorded *equal*, not preferential, status and dignity.

Thus, there is currently a movement afoot in a number of states to enact "Personhood Amendments" to the respective constitutions as a prelude to amending the U.S. Constitution to correct the perceived flaws in the 14th Amendment. One obvious response, of course, is to point out that, given the proper understanding of the basis and form of the United States government, we don't need to amend the Constitution on this point.

This does not mean that the "Personhood Movement" is useless, wrong-headed, or anything other than a sign that "the people" are becoming sufficiently concerned about the loss of civil rights to organize in social justice and direct their efforts to the reform of the institutions of the common good. This is what Alexis de Tocqueville described as the quintessential characteristic of American life in the 1830s. According to the author of *Democracy in America*, people did not wait for the State to act, but took matters into their own hands as a matter of course, organized, and addressed social problems by acting directly on the relevant institutions without interference from the State. This sort of thing was so pervasive de Tocqueville declared that in America the federal government hardly seemed to govern at all.[1]

The mere fact that the Personhood Movement exists thus suggests — strongly — that there is a growing public perception that something is terribly wrong in how the United States Supreme Court has interpreted the Constitution, the second most important founding document of the United States. The most important document, of course, is the Declaration of Independence, which, while not itself law, gives context to and justifies the Constitution. It would be a serious mistake for "the powers that be" to conclude that, because (in their opinion) "Personhood Amendments" have little chance of being enacted, the movement can safely be ignored.

---

[1] Alexis de Tocqueville, "The Principle of the Sovereignty of the People of America," *Democracy in America*, I.iv.

If nothing else, the Personhood Movement focuses attention on the way the Supreme Court, in what dissenting Justice Byron R. White declared an exercise of "raw judicial power," has apparently pushed some extremely creative reinterpretations onto the Constitution in furtherance of questionable political ends. The movement alone may be sufficient, without managing to get any state or federal amendments enacted, to cause our nation's leaders to wake up to the fact that something is seriously wrong in their basic understanding of the role of the State. This, in and of itself, may be enough to persuade our leaders to take steps to correct matters.

What needs amendment and correction, then, is not the wording of the Constitution or any Amendment, but the legal philosophy and moral orientation of the justices on the Supreme Court. There is, after all, no guarantee that, in the event a Personhood Amendment is adopted, the U.S. Supreme Court will change its thinking and interpret a new amendment differently from the understanding the Court has already forced on the rather clear wording of the 14th Amendment by ignoring the 9th and 10th Amendments, leaving the situation unchanged.

Is there, however, a way to change the thinking of the Court and reorient its thinking and philosophy to something more consistent with the natural law basis on which the United States was founded?

12. Public Opinion

In the previous chapter we discovered that the current push for "Personhood Amendments" in a number of states is a necessary and salutary effort in the struggle to restore the social order to something more conformable to the principles of the natural law, and thus to human nature. The problem is that there are groups that seem determined to remake humanity in their own image, and force their vision onto everyone else, using the coercive power of the State to accomplish this end. Unfortunately, these include both Pro-Life and Pro-Choice groups, which counters, to some extent, the effort to find a common ground between the two.

Part of the problem with reorienting people's thinking is the fixed idea many people have that the State can do anything, or (more accurately) that we can use the State to gain whatever ends we desire. Further, the individual is helpless in the face of unjust social structures. This is an extremely naïve view not only of the role of the State and of the place of the person in the State, but also of the power that the State and the law actually have to change attitudes and behavior — that which constitutional scholar Albert Venn Dicey (1835-1922), noted for his emphasis on the "rule of law,"[1] called "public opinion."

As Dicey pointed out in his landmark study on the sociology of law, the less-than-snappily titled if extremely erudite and profound (and out of print, except for what reviewers have called an overpriced and very bad edition) *Lectures on the Relation Between Law and Public Opinion in England During the Nineteenth Century* (1905), the effectiveness of any law depends on how the public receives it. That is, how "public opinion" agrees with and

---

[1] http://en.wikipedia.org/wiki/Albert_Venn_Dicey

perceives a particular law affects the understanding and interpretation of that law and other institutions, as well as its enforcement.

Dicey's book, by the way, is an excellent accompaniment to Alexis de Tocqueville's sociological analysis, *Democracy in America* (Volume I, 1835; Volume II, 1840). Not surprisingly, both de Tocqueville and Dicey were great admirers of the United States. Both, however, pinpointed possible dangers in the American system. These have, in large measure, made serious inroads on the natural rights of life, liberty, property, and pursuit of happiness, the protection of which presumably constitutes the chief reason and justification for the United States. For de Tocqueville, the danger lay in false notions of equality. For Dicey the concern was the corruption he saw inherent in party politics.

Dicey's conclusion was that if people are prepared to accept a new law, there is a high likelihood that the law will be obeyed and have the intended result. If, however, people are not prepared to accept a new law, then there is a good probability that the law will not be obeyed, or will have effects sometimes the exact opposite of what was intended. The best examples of the latter case in the United States are the Fugitive Slave Act of 1850[2] and Prohibition,[3] both of which were widely disobeyed and actually advanced the activities they were intended to counter.

In social justice, of course, the primary power to change and reform our institutions rests not with the State, but with individual people. This, however, can be misunderstood as a statement of individualism or anarchy. On the contrary, as Rev. William J. Ferree, S.M., Ph.D., makes clear in *Introduction to Social Justice*,[4] or-

---

[2] http://en.wikipedia.org/wiki/Fugitive_Slave_Law_of_1850

[3] http://en.wikipedia.org/wiki/Prohibition

[4] William J. Ferree, S.M., Ph.D., *Introduction to Social Justice*. Arlington, Virginia: Center for Economic and Social Justice, 1997.

dinary, everyday people have the power to act directly on the common good. The common good is the network of institutions within which we as human persons exercise our natural rights and thereby acquire and develop virtue.

It is not, however, as individuals *per se* that we have the power to act directly on the institutions of the common good, including our laws, customs, and traditions. Instead, it is only as members of organized groups that we can act *socially* — and remain, at the same time, fully differentiated *individuals* within the organized structures of institutions. As Edmund Burke declared in *Thoughts on the Cause of Present Discontents* (1770): "When bad men combine, the good must associate; else they will fall one by one, an unpitied sacrifice in a contemptible struggle." (Burke did *not* say, "All that is necessary for evil to triumph is for good men to do nothing," an individualistic rephrasing of the more socially just approach Burke described.)

This, the apparent paradox of social justice, explains how we can retain our individual identity and human dignity, and at the same time act in accordance with our social nature. As Aristotle reminds us, "man is by nature a political animal." That still leaves us, however, with the problem of protecting each person's essential human dignity in the face of such egregious misunderstanding and misinterpretation of basic principles of the natural moral law and the United States Constitution as exemplified by *Roe v. Wade.*

If, as we have seen, public opinion appears to be ranged against any limitations on the presumed right to an abortion (as if a right could ever be exercised without *any* limitation), how do we, as seemingly helpless individuals, organize and change public opinion so that public opinion no longer regards abortion as a right, and that a law making abortion illegal — if it would even be necessary at that point — would be effective instead of destructive of the social order?

Part III: The Choice

13. Can We Disobey the Law?

As a practical matter, and leaving out ethical considerations, if abortion were to be outlawed tomorrow, it is highly likely that the law would be flouted to an even greater extent than the Fugitive Slave Act or Prohibition. Going contrary to what many people, justly or unjustly, have become convinced is a right is a recipe for social disaster on a massive scale. This is why Aquinas counseled that (assuming that we are not personally obliged to do evil) obedience even to the worst of laws is required, if breaking the law or refusing to obey it would cause the situation to get worse, cause massive social upheaval, or even the destruction of the social order itself.

In *De Regimine Principum*, the "Angelic Doctor" (as Aquinas is sometimes called), related the story of the tyrant Dionysus of Syracuse who, at a time when he seemed to be reviled and hated by everyone, was surprised to come across an old woman praying fervently to the gods for his safety and long life.[1] Naturally enough, Dionysus asked why, when everyone else was hoping for his early demise, she was doing exactly the opposite. The old woman explained that when she was a young girl, a terrible tyrant oppressed the land, and everyone prayed for deliverance. The tyrant died, and was replaced with a worse one, and so on, until now, near the end of her life, Dionysus, the worst of the lot, seized power. That being her experience, she now prayed that he would last long in power, for she couldn't take anyone worse.

In moral philosophy (ethics), the only time we are permitted to disobey even a bad law is when the law requires us, individually and personally, to act contrary to our consciences — always assuming, of course, that we have

---

[1] Aquinas, *De Regimine Principum*, I.6.xliv.

- 57 -

formed our consciences in accordance with nature. Co-
erced obedience in that case would constitute an offense
against our human dignity. This is the same human dignity that the State, as guardian of the common good, is
required to safeguard. The State does this by preserving
and protecting the institutional environment within
which we as moral creatures acquire and develop virtue
and so become more fully human.

Pro-Choice advocates, whether or not they realize this
principle on a conscious level, have been quick to exploit it
to the disadvantage of the Pro-Life movement. Pro-Choice
advocates are in the forefront of those who demand obedience to the law . . . as long as it is a law with which they
agree. Logically, of course, consistent with their line of
reasoning that *Roe v. Wade* established abortion on demand as the law of the land, simply passing a law to the
contrary would end the matter. If they acted in a manner
consistent with their expressed principle that the State in
the person of the United States Supreme Court creates
the law and thereby determines what is right and wrong,
Pro-Choice advocates would defend the outlawing of abortion with the same vigor, even fanaticism with which they
have defended the presumed right to abortion, similarly
established by law.

Simply passing a law, as we have seen, however, does
nothing if people are not prepared to accept or obey the
law. In the event a law prohibiting abortion on demand
were to be passed, many people would act contrary to
their stated principles, and disobey it, despite their previous insistence that the law as established by the State is
absolute and sacred. To believe otherwise is to be living in
a fantasy world.

There is, however, a very effective tactic that has yet to
be tried, one that is based not on passing a new law, but
on demanding full and impartial enforcement of what
Pro-Choice advocates insist is the current law of the land.
In one sense, of course, this could be viewed as a very
clever turning of the tables on the Pro-Choice position.

Ultimately, however, it is not some kind of legal chicanery, but a simple demand for justice — and on the terms set and the ground defined by the Pro-Choice movement.

14. What is a Right?

As we noted in the previous chapter, simply passing a law to prohibit abortion or adopting a Constitutional amendment protecting personality (which already exists in the 14th Amendment) would in all likelihood be ineffective. If what A. V. Dicey called "public opinion" does not support the law, the law will either not be obeyed, or will have a substantially different effect than what was intended. For any legislation affecting abortion to be effective, there must be some sort of common ground on which Pro-Choice and Pro-Life adherents can meet and agree.

Some people have complained that using the term "Pro-Choice" is both misleading and concedes too much to the opposition. That may be the case, but (as we shall see presently) it is a meaningless concession that has the potential to provide the basis for a quantum advance for the Pro-Life movement — if Pro-Choice advocates are sincere in their beliefs, especially the existence of a *right* to free choice, and honest (or at least consistent) in their application of the principle.

First, we have to realize of what a right consists. A *right* is the power to do or not do some act in relation to others. The existence of a right (which implies the functioning of justice) necessarily involves a correlative *duty*. A duty is the obligation to do some act in relation to the right holder. Thus, a right to a free choice regarding a specific act means that someone has the power to choose to do or not do that act, with the choice being free from coercion or undue influence exercised by others.

The right of a free choice regarding a specific act necessarily includes the right of a free choice to participate materially or *not* participate materially in assisting others in doing or not doing that act. For example, if slavery were legal, someone could freely choose to own a slave.

The prospective slave owner could not, however, by any means force someone who does not choose to own a slave either to own a slave, to assist the prospective slave owner in any material way in procuring a slave, or to promote slavery or slave owning.

The State has a monopoly over the instruments of coercion to force compliance with its will. This, of course, must be in accordance with the general consent of the governed, as long as the general consent of the governed or the interpretation and application of that will does not violate either a natural right held by everyone (regardless of their expressed will) or the rights of a minority — even a minority of one.

Given the legality of slavery, the State's obligation would therefore be limited to permitting people to own slaves, and to passing and enforcing laws regulating the sale, purchase, and possession of slaves (*e.g.*, acceptable treatment, working conditions, compensation, *etc.*). The State would be exceeding its authority if it were to force non-slave owners or abolitionists to own slaves, promote slavery, or to subsidize slavery through the tax system. These are all actions that involve either explicit or implied coercion on the part of the State, and thus an exercise of undue influence or actual threat forcing people to act contrary to their consciences.

We can make the same observations regarding the wage system prevalent under both capitalism and socialism. Given the existence of the wage system, an arrangement that some people have described as a condition of "wage slavery," the State's obligation is limited to permitting people to subsist exclusively on wages, and to passing and enforcing laws regulating hiring, termination, and terms of employment (*e.g.*, acceptable treatment, working conditions, compensation, *etc.*). The State exceeds its authority if it forces people to work solely for wages, promotes the wage system over other economic arrangements, subsidizes the wage system, or prohibits or inhibits ownership of the means of production by anyone —

thereby establishing a condition of society that Hilaire Belloc called "the Servile State" in his 1912 book of the same title.

15. No Way Out?

As we have seen in previous chapters, the Pro-Choice position seems to have the Pro-Life position completely boxed in. In substantiation, we have the clear teaching in moral philosophy that if a bad law, even a very bad law, does not force us personally to do evil, we must permit the law to continue, if our taking action would reasonably be expected to disrupt significantly or destroy the social order. Social order — the network of institutions known as the common good[1] — is such a great good that we must allow even incredible evil to continue if stopping the evil would destroy or materially harm the social order. To put an end to the matter, we are constantly told that abortion on demand is the law of the land. It must be permitted and supported without question with all the resources of the State and the people.

Regardless of the shoddy legal and social reasoning behind such assertions, the Pro-Life movement, and (evidently) the Personhood Movement to some degree appear to have accepted this understanding of the situation. Consequently (so the reasoning seems to go), if the law can be changed, then the coercive power of the State and all the resources of the nation can be used to stop abortion rather

---

[1] "It [the common good] includes the sum or sociological integration of all the civic conscience, political virtues and sense of right and liberty, of all the activity, material prosperity and spiritual riches, of unconsciously operative hereditary wisdom, of moral rectitude, justice, friendship, happiness, virtue and heroism in the individual lives of its members. For these things all are, in a certain measure, *communicable* and so revert to each member, helping him to perfect his life and liberty of person. They all constitute the good human life of the multitude." Jacques Maritain, *The Person and the Common Good*. Notre Dame, Indiana: University of Notre Dame Press, 1966, 52-53.

than protect and promote it. This understanding ignores both political and social reality, and the act of social justice.

As we previously noted, simply passing a law — whether in the form of an Amendment to the Constitution or a Supreme Court decision — does nothing to change a situation if people don't want it to be changed. Prohibition, for example, while intended to eliminate the presumed scourge of drunkenness and all the crime and sin associated with the consumption of alcohol, caused massive upheaval in the social order. Public opinion was opposed to Prohibition to such an extent that conventional government and rule of law virtually disappeared in some areas of the country.

The Supreme Court's decision in *Scott v. Sandford*[2] that upheld the right to own slaves everywhere in the United States and effectively overturned the Missouri Compromise of 1820[3] was itself overturned within five years by the bloodiest war in American history. The Supreme Court's role in exacerbating the conflict between Pro-Slavery adherents and Abolitionists in the Dred Scott decision, combined with the presumed economic necessity of chattel slavery argued in David Christy's 1855 book *Cotton is King*, has not been adequately studied or appreciated as a direct cause of the Civil War.

The situation seems hopeless — which is precisely what it is . . . at least from the standpoint of individual and individualistic efforts to solve the problem. To illustrate this, let's paraphrase a passage from Rev. William Ferree's, *Introduction to Social Justice*,[4] substituting "abortion" for "honesty."

> The question is: What can Jane Jones do as an individual? She might, for instance, decide to give the community "a good example" of a Pro-Life approach to

---

[2] 60 U.S. (19 How.) 393 (1857)
[3] http://en.wikipedia.org/wiki/Missouri_Compromise
[4] Ferree, *op. cit.*, 44-45.

the problem. That is, she could refuse to obtain an abortion, regardless of the circumstances surrounding her situation (*e.g.*, rape, incest, lack of adequate or secure income, social embarrassment, *etc.*), and allow herself to be showcased as an exemplar of adherence to Pro-Life principles. This sounds good; but, remembering that what is wrong with that community is that everyone considers it *normal* to have an abortion under these and similar circumstances, we might readily calculate the chances that Jane Jones' heroic adherence to Pro-Life principles would have of reforming the community. When she refuses to go along with the dictates of public opinion, she will be idolized briefly by a relatively small segment of the population, vilified and ridiculed in the media, and shunned by family and friends for making the wrong choice. As soon as the next *cause célèbre* comes along, she will be forgotten, having lost in the interim her job, her reputation, and virtually all hope of a normal life in society. It is unlikely that her example will attract many followers among women seeking abortions or men promoting them. Her mistake was to attack a *social* evil with only *individual* means.

Part IV: Social Justice

16. The Way Out

In the previous chapter we noted that, according to Reverend William Ferree, eulogized on his death in 1985 as "America's greatest social philosopher," even super-heroic *individual* virtue has little if any chance of ameliorating a *social* evil. As the paraphrase of the passage from *Introduction to Social Justice* pointed out, "Her [Jane Jones'] mistake was to attack a *social* evil with only *individual* means." The question becomes, "How should she have gone about it?"

The Personhood Movement and the Pro-Life movement could, of course, continue to do exactly what they are doing: stage public demonstrations and distribute propaganda (in the good sense) with the end of enacting a law or adopting a constitutional amendment the object of which is to prevent abortion. We have seen, however, that simply passing a law or even amending the Constitution is, absent public support, ineffectual and can even bring about greater evils than the one presumably being eliminated.

The ineffectiveness of the usual approach (aside from its implicit denial of individual sovereignty within the social order and its reliance on the coercive power of the State to impose desired ends) is evident once we internalize the basic principles of social justice. Primarily, as Father Ferree points out in his unfinished manuscript, *Forty Years After . . . A Second Call to Battle* (c. 1985), such demonstrations, necessary and useful as they might be to raise public consciousness of an issue and even in saving infants' and mothers' lives on an individual basis, all have one fatal weakness: they are all inevitably demands that *somebody else* do something, *i.e.*, stop having, performing, supporting, or promoting abortions. The demonstrator is, socially speaking, completely ineffective, although left

with a feeling of great virtue and vast superiority over
other, less enlightened people who "don't get it." The institution of abortion as a socially acceptable thing is left
unchanged, except perhaps to strengthen the resolve of
Pro-Choice extremists to resist the efforts of the "anti-
abortion terrorists" to take away their right to choose.

We find the answer to this seemingly insoluble situation in the laws and characteristics of social justice. As
Father Ferree explains in *Introduction to Social Justice,*

> Another corollary of this characteristic of Social Jus-
> tice (that it is never finished) is that it embraces a
> *rigid obligation.* In the past when it was not seen very
> clearly how the duty of reform would fall upon the in-
> dividual conscience, the idea became widespread that
> reform was a kind of special vocation, like that to the
> priesthood, or the religious life. It was all very good
> for those people who liked that sort of thing, but if one
> did not like that sort of thing, he left it alone.

> All that is changed! Since we know that everyone,
> even the weakest and youngest of human beings, can
> work *directly* on the Common Good at the level where
> he lives, and since each one "has the duty" to reorgan-
> ize his own natural medium of life whenever it makes
> the practice of individual virtue difficult or impossi-
> ble, then every single person must face the direct and
> strict obligation of reorganizing his life and the life
> around him, so that the individual perfection both of
> himself and of his immediate neighbors will become
> possible. This idea should not be taken alone, it
> should be held only in conjunction with the character-
> istics we have already seen, namely, that one cannot
> practice Social Justice alone as an individual, but only
> with others; and that the realization of Social Justice
> takes time.[1]

---

[1] *Ibid.,* 52.

That is, when individual virtue cannot function, or does so only partially or inadequately, the solution is to organize with others. It then becomes possible to work directly not on the specific problem itself, but on the surrounding institutions of the common good that are "allowing" the problem to continue or, in extreme cases, causing the problem.

In this manner we can organize and work to establish an economically — and thus politically — just society, based on four essential pillars:

- A limited economic role for the State,

- Free and open markets as the best means of determining just wages, just prices, and just profits,

- Restoration of the rights of private property, especially in corporate equity, and (the "fatal omission" from virtually all economic systems today)

- Widespread direct ownership of the means of production.

With respect to abortion and the effort to get the fetus recognized as a person in conformity with the principles of the natural moral law on which the United States is founded, this is a two-step process. That is what we will cover in the next chapter.

17. Common Ground

In the previous chapter we noted that individual or individualistic approaches to fundamental social change are, absent some miracle, usually ineffective. That is because *individual* methods are generally useless in addressing a *social* situation. We are, however, left with a serious problem. It is contrary to the principles of natural law on which this country is explicitly based to force anyone to participate in an act that person regards as evil. Forcing citizens to participate in a morally repugnant act is, in moral philosophy, legitimate grounds for changing rulers, even (in extreme cases) the form of government.[1]

Nevertheless, we have to acknowledge that, in the present state of society, unilaterally abolishing legalized abortion is not practicable, even if it could be done tomorrow. Such a move would, in all likelihood, cause even more immediate harm to the social order than that inflicted at present by abortion and other activities that the Pro-Life movement considers related. As Reverend William Ferree points out in *Introduction to Social Justice*, the primary law of social justice is that the common good must be kept inviolate.[2] As "America's greatest social philosopher" explains,

> To attack or to endanger the Common Good in order attain some private end, no matter how good or how necessary this latter may be in its own order, is social injustice and is wrong. The Common Good is *not* a means for any particular interests; it is *not* a bargaining point in any private quarrel whatsoever; it is *not* a

---

[1] Aquinas, *De Regimine Principum*, I.vi; Bellarmine, *De Rom. Pont. Eccl. Monarchia*, Lib. I, Cap. VI. Nota quarta. *De Laicis*, Cap. VI; also *Recognitio, Libri Tertii De Laicis*.
[2] Ferree, *op. cit.*, 35.

pressure that one may legitimately exercise to obtain any private ends. It is a good so great that very frequently private rights — even inviolable private rights — cannot be exercised until it is safeguarded.[3]

This is not to say that continued legalized abortion will not inflict even greater harm on the common good in the long term. It is a case of dealing with the lesser — that is, the most immediate — of two evils (maintaining order in society in the face of obvious, even horrifying injustice), not an admission that abortion is somehow a good. Direct participation in abortion is always evil, but at present the anticipated evil of the serious disruption or destruction of the social order should abortion be outlawed is of more immediate concern.

There is, however, a possible political "common ground" that can exist in the debate. This gives us a basis for achieving the only possible middle ground between the Pro-Life and the Pro-Choice positions: a Pro-Life economic agenda, a means of exercising rights without coercion or undue influence from any quarter. If abortion supporters are truly "Pro-Choice," then they should be the strongest supporters of a Pro-Life economic agenda designed to remove entirely any economic pressure to procure an abortion. They would thereby bring an end to the undue influence on free choice exerted by economic institutions.

Consistent with that, Pro-Choice advocates should be in the forefront of the effort to end all government support for abortions, direct or indirect. They would thereby take away the implied political and social endorsement for abortion. Such tacit approval can obviate "free" choice even more effectively than economic forces. A fully consistent Pro-Choice position would be to deny any and all deductions for taxpayers who give money to support or procure abortions. This is because tax deductibility involves a substantial degree of government support, as well as pro-

---

[3] *Ibid.*

viding what amounts to a subsidy that must be made up by increasing taxes paid by all taxpayers.[4]

In view of the political realities of the situation, the Pro-Life movement may be able to give a reassurance to the Pro-Choice movement that, consistent with the democratic process, abortion will not be criminalized until such time as an overwhelming consensus is reached that this should, indeed, be the case. This is, to all intents and purposes, a meaningless concession. Such a law would be ineffective anyway until and unless an overwhelming consensus is reached, something of which the Pro-Choice movement should be fully aware.

Still, should the Pro-Choice movement balk at eliminating all forms of government support (financial and otherwise) for abortion, the Pro-Life movement must seek legal redress. As we have seen, it is both inconsistent and unconstitutional for the Pro-Choice movement to demand the right to choose whether or not to have an abortion, or support or promote abortion, and yet at the same time deny others the right to choose whether or not to pay for that abortion through the use of their tax monies. A challenge to federal, state and local government support in any form for abortions should, on legal grounds, have a good chance of becoming law — to say nothing of saving massive amounts of money that, in these times of economic turmoil, could certainly be put to better use.

Failing that, an option that might be considered is a "tax revolt," keeping in mind that such action cannot be recommended except as a last resort against a State that has, in effect, become a tyranny — and deciding whether the State is tyrannical is *not* a matter of private judgment

---

[4] This in no way endangers the tax-free status of religious institutions. Religious institutions constitute a discrete society over which the State cannot legitimately claim jurisdiction. The State cannot tax religion or religious activities without interfering with the civil right to freedom of religion. In any event, the right of choice is construed as a civil right, that is, a right in civil society, not a religious doctrine.

or personal opinion. If the "best men" in the community (as Aquinas calls them) have, after due consideration and reflection, determined the State is tyrannical, then changing rulers or the form of government — or withholding taxes — may be the only recourse.

For example, and although the position was equivocal (being based on private judgment about the morality of the action), during the Vietnam War, a number of people either refused to pay taxes at all, or withheld a portion of their taxes. Many of them ended up in prison, but if the 51% of the population that, according to a recent Gallup Poll describe themselves as "Pro-Life" refused to pay unjust taxes, the government would be forced to capitulate. Such a move, of course, would be feasible only after all legal means were exhausted, including bringing the case to the Supreme Court, which, if it wishes to retain its credibility, could not rationally allow free choice to obtain an abortion while denying free choice to pay for it.

Removal of all forms of government support at all levels for abortion in any way shape or form is only a part of the solution, although it would constitute in and of itself a major victory. Such an effort should, in the interests of equal rights for all, be led by the American Civil Liberties Union. The ACLU would otherwise have to admit publicly that the rights they demand for their preferred groups and causes do not, in fact, apply equally to all. The ACLU would put themselves in the position of advocating not a *right*, but a *privilege*.[5]

Further, removing all forms of government support at all levels would convince a great many people, trained to look to the State as the arbiter of right and wrong, that abortion might not be quite as fundamental a right as Pro-Choice adherents insist. Removing all State support would go a long way toward persuading people that all human beings, including fetuses (Latin for "unborn hu-

---

[5] The correlative of right is duty, but the correlative of privilege is "no right."

man being") are persons within the natural law context of the United States Constitution, and the Declaration of Independence that (while not itself law) gives context to the Constitution.

As a result, the economic (and thus political) system would conform more closely to the "principles of economic justice" of binary economics: 1) Distribution, 2) Participation, and 3) Harmony or "social justice."[6]

The "Principle of Distribution" is that, just as the creation of new money must be tied directly through the institution of private property to the present value of existing and future marketable goods and services, everyone who participates in the production of wealth should receive a share of the production proportionate to the value of his or her input to production.[7]

The "Principle of Participation" is that everyone has a "natural right" to life. This necessarily means that everyone has a right to maintain and preserve his or her life by all legitimate means — especially the right to obtain subsistence by participating in the production of wealth, individually or in free association with others.

The "Principle of Harmony" is that when our institutions become distorted or ineffective to the point that they no longer assist us in acquiring and developing virtue, we must organize, restructure our institutions, and bring these institutions back into reasonable conformity with the demands of the natural law.[8]

---

[6] *The Capitalist Manifesto, op. cit.*, 66-86.

[7] *Ibid.*, 67.

[8] Norman G. Kurland's paper, "A New Look at Prices and Money: The Kelsonian Binary Model for Achieving Rapid Growth Without Inflation," *The Journal of Socio-Economics*, Vol. 30, 495-515, studies the overall anticipated systemic effect of applying the principles of binary economics throughout an economy.

Part V: The Economic Agenda

18. Right to Life = Right to Living

As we saw in the previous chapter, the Pro-Life movement can achieve a great victory simply by insisting that the presumed right to choice be applied consistently and justly. People should be secure in their right not to be forced to have, promote, or support abortions in any way, especially by the use of their tax monies. Neither the Supreme Court of the United States nor the Pro-Choice movement can sustain any argument in favor of continued State support of any kind for abortion.

There is, however, one remaining thing that must be done. The charge of hypocrisy has already been leveled at the Pro-Life movement. This is based on the allegation that people in the movement care only what happens to the fetus, not about the quality of life of the baby once born. This is a legitimate criticism up to a point, but hardly of the magnitude to be termed hypocritical.

The adoption of a Pro-Life economic agenda, first for the United States, and then the world would not only remove the charge of hypocrisy from the Pro-Life movement, it would in large measure remove any and all economic justification for abortion. There is a program that should be investigated that may have the potential to open up the opportunity for each family to generate income sufficient to meet common domestic needs adequately. The program is Capital Homesteading for every citizen, from the book with the same title.[1] Capital Homesteading is a detailed, life-supporting application of the principles of binary economics.

---

[1] Norman G. Kurland, Dawn K. Brohawn, and Michael D. Greaney, *Capital Homesteading for Every Citizen: A Just Free Market Solution for Saving Social Security*. Arlington, Virginia: Economic Justice Media, 2004.

While there are other approaches, we believe that Capital Homesteading is, all things considered, the best, most consistent, and most "person-centered" approach to economic development we've yet come across. We are, however, open to suggestions about improvements and even other proposals that can demonstrate as close a consistency to the natural moral law as Capital Homesteading.

A couple of *caveats* need to be inserted here. First, these chapters can only give the broadest and sketchiest outline of Capital Homesteading. If the concept interests you at all, or if you think you find flaws in what is said here, go first to the CESJ website, www.cesj.org, and read up on the subject.

Second (and this may be even more controversial than the claim to have found a common ground with the Pro-Choice movement), be aware that Capital Homesteading uses a different definition of "money" than the one with which you may be familiar. This is something of which we ourselves only recently realized the full import. Briefly, Capital Homesteading — consistent with CESJ's Aristotelian/Thomist natural law orientation — defines money by its nature and proper use, not as a creature of positive law, that is, of direct State action.

In other words, CESJ understands "money" in ontological terms of what it *is*, instead of what it happens to *do* or (more immediately) can be forced to do. The former is based on nature, the latter on will — usually that of the State, which thereby tries to take on the divine aspect of being able to determine reality. This latter is the view of the Keynesian, Monetarist, and Austrian schools of economics.[2]

CESJ defines "money" as anything that can be used in settlement of a debt; the "medium of exchange." You don't ordinarily need anybody's permission, especially that of

---

[2] See, *e.g.*, John Maynard Keynes, *A Treatise on Money, Volume I: The Pure Theory of Money*. New York: Harcourt, Brace and Company, 1930, 4.

the State, to trade what you have for that which someone else has. As Jean-Baptiste Say explained in his refutation of the scarcity-based economics of Reverend Thomas Malthus, you don't make your purchases of what others produce with "money," *per se*, but with what you produce by means of your labor or your capital. "Money" is simply a "social tool" — a medium — to facilitate transactions. If some people cannot sell all they produce, it is because other people are not producing.[3]

This natural law definition of "money" is implicit in the tenets of the "Banking School," as well as in the work of Dr. Harold Moulton (notably in his 1935 classic, *The Formation of Capital*), the binary economics of Louis Kelso and Mortimer Adler, and even the venerable Adam Smith in *The Wealth of Nations* (1776). This is emphasized in the subtitle of the second book Kelso and Adler co-authored in 1961, *The New Capitalists*: "A Proposal to Free Economic Growth from the Slavery of Savings."

Finally, be aware that Kelso and Adler made two "mistakes" in the title of their book. One, they carried the vague term "capitalism" over from their first collaboration, *The Capitalist Manifesto* (1958). In *The Capitalist Manifesto* they explain that by "capitalism" they mean an economic system in which capital, not labor, is the predominant factor of production. This is less than helpful, for the definition also fits socialist economies. As Chesterton remarked, "If the use of capital is capitalism, then everything is capitalism."[4]

Two (though this is not really an error), the phrase "Slavery of Savings" implies hostility toward or a rejection of savings. On reading *The New Capitalists*, however, we quickly discover that the "slavery" to which Kelso and Adler refer is dependence on *existing* accumulations of savings to finance capital formation. Dependence on *past* savings or reductions in current consumption restricts

---

[3] Jean-Baptiste Say, *Letters to Mr. Malthus* (1821), 2.
[4] G. K. Chesterton, *The Outline of Sanity*, 1927, Ch. 1.

capital ownership to those who can afford to save, or who receive redistributed capital from the State (in which case they cannot truly be said to *own* that wealth).

What Kelso and Adler proposed was to replace *past* savings with *future* savings. That is, instead of cutting consumption and accumulating in order to invest, the process is reversed so that investment in new capital generates its own repayment — a basic principle of finance. It is no longer (and never actually was) necessary to cut current consumption. Instead, by creating money backed by the present value of the future stream of income to be generated by the newly formed capital, current consumption levels can be maintained, even increased, at the same time that income is generated to repay the financing of the very capital that generates the income.

By *future* savings, we do not mean *forced* or *involuntary* savings, terms which have a completely different — and much more complicated — meaning in most modern schools of economics. It is so complicated and contradictory that it would be counterproductive even to try to explain it here. Admittedly we have, confusingly, used "future" and "forced" savings as synonyms in the past — and might in the future (nobody's perfect) — but the reader should be aware that there is, in fact, a significant difference between the *future* savings concept in binary economics, and the *forced* savings theory in Keynesian, Monetarist, and Austrian schools of economics.

Thus, to understand Capital Homesteading, keep in mind that the proposal uses a different understanding of money than is usual today, and that it rejects Malthusian concepts of scarcity as invalid.[5]

---

[5] See the analysis in Joseph A. Schumpeter, *History of Economic Analysis*. New York: Oxford University Press, 1954, 579-580.

19. On Labor and Capital

In the previous chapter we discovered that, to understand Capital Homesteading (particularly as a Pro-Life economic agenda) we have to reject outdated notions of money and credit, as well as discredited Malthusian concepts of scarcity. Once we separate the in-depth thinkers from the not-so-in-depth thinkers and get over that admittedly revolutionary *Pons Asinorum*, we can get on to the even more radical ("radical" in terms of today's ossified thinking, that is) particulars of Capital Homesteading.

Throughout history the rich and powerful have owned the things that produced the world's wealth. When land and people produced wealth, the rich and powerful owned land and people. Today what produces most of the wealth are land and technology — "capital," that is, non-human (non-person) *things*. This is why Kelso and Adler (mistakenly, in our opinion) characterized the modern economy as *capitalist*. In particular, technologies such as machinery, robots, rentable structures, and advanced information systems are replacing people at their workplaces and threatening their family incomes.

Obviously, then, the people who own the land and the technology (productive capital) are today's "rich and powerful." Due to flawed thinking about money, credit, and scarcity, many people accept the concentration of ownership of the means of production as a given. Unfortunately, this results in a state of society in which too few people own income-producing wealth (capital), and too many people own nothing. The result is a society in which many people owe more than they own, and the great mass of people are utterly dependent either on a private elite (as in capitalism), or a State elite (as in socialism). The tragedy is that many otherwise thoughtful people reach the

conclusion that this situation is somehow normal or consistent with the natural moral law.

The bottom line is that anyone is economically vulnerable if he or she doesn't own — as private property — a
just and adequate capital stake in the land and technology that produce most of today's wealth. To make matters
worse, economic power is tied closely to political power.
Political power comes from property (the rights and powers of ownership) and the means to acquire and possess
private property in the means of production: capital. In
today's global economy, the most significant forms of capital are advanced technologies. These can be and in many
cases are directly owned, but most capital today is owned
through unique social tools called corporations — the
ownership of which (due to how capital formation is financed[1]) is highly concentrated in the hands of a very few
people.

When ownership is concentrated, power is concentrated. This is why today a few people are very powerful,
and most people are virtually powerless. The wealth-
producing power of an individual worker — as "pure labor," *sans* technology — has not increased appreciably
since the dawn of time. Poor people and most non-
property-owning workers can only produce insecure subsistence incomes from their jobs. Some people, however,
profit from the work that technology can do by owning
shares in the companies that use that technology. These
people become rich and powerful because they own the
things (capital) that produce most of our wealth.

In a democratic and just economy everyone should
have an equal opportunity and equal access to the means
to own shares in companies that use advanced technology.
The U.S. economy, for example, should have programs
that lift artificial tax and credit barriers to help every
American become an owner of American Industry. Every

---

[1] See Hilaire Belloc's analysis in *The Servile State* (1912), § 4.

family could then earn income from jobs and income from capital that each family member would own.

The question is, how?

Today many people, even the poor, can purchase consumer items such as cars, television sets, clothing, and homes on credit. These purchases are not, however, "capital": income-earning property. Borrowing for such things makes the debtor more economically vulnerable than otherwise. Meanwhile, every year before the current economic debacle America added about $2 trillion worth of new productive assets in both the public sector and private sector, or approximately $7,000 for every man, woman, and child. The way we finance these new assets creates few new owners and widens the gap between the "haves" and the "have-nots."

Constrained by bad definitions of money and other flawed institutions, the usual solution takes two forms. One, capitalism is "socialized," and the State takes over control of the economy indirectly by mandating prices, wages, interest rates, and so on. Two, the State takes over direct control of the economy — socialism by any name. This can be done through subsidies and bailouts of businesses considered too big to fail, or by taking over actual ownership (control) of companies.

Whether by socializing capitalism or by implementing socialism outright, those in authority (usually the State, but it could be a private elite) circumvent institutional flaws by redistributing existing wealth. This is not only ineffective and counterproductive, it is inadequate even within its own framework and works only for a short time. Redistribution is usually carried out either directly, indirectly through the tax system, or by manipulating the currency through inflation or deflation. The specific method depends on whether the State wishes to favor debtors or creditors, respectively.

There is, however, an alternative to the current system that is neither socialism nor capitalism. This "Just Third Way" would be a free enterprise economy, generating private sector profits — but with ownership of the new growth systematically flowing to every individual citizen. With access to capital credit repayable with the full pretax earnings of the capital itself, everyone could gain ownership in America's expanding technological frontier. We wouldn't have to take away wealth from those who already own capital, or rely on an allegedly beneficent and all-powerful State to distribute largesse to the presumably needy and those deemed sufficiently worthy.

One application of the principles of binary economics[2] found in the Just Third Way is called "Capital Homesteading," as in the title of the book, *Capital Homesteading for Every Citizen*. The Capital Homesteading concept has been developed into a specific proposal called the "Capital Homestead Act."

---

[2] "Binary" means "consisting of two parts." Binary economics divides the factors of production into two all-inclusive categories — the human ("labor"), and the non-human ("capital"). The central tenet of binary economics is that there are two components to productive output and to income: (1) that generated by human labor, and (2) that generated by capital. Classical economic theory, on the other hand, regards all output and income to be derived from labor whose productivity is enhanced by capital. The principles of binary economics are found in the two books coauthored by Louis Kelso and Mortimer Adler, *The Capitalist Manifesto*. New York: Random House, 1958, and *The New Capitalists*. New York: Random House, 1961. An in-depth treatment of binary economics can be found in Robert Ashford and Rodney Shakespeare, *Binary Economics: The New Paradigm*. Lanham, Maryland: University Press of America, 1999.

20. Capital Homesteading

As we have tried to make clear in this book, the outlook for the Pro-Life movement is far from hopeless. While the *individual* is frequently helpless to effect change in social situations, the remedy of *social* justice is open to every single human being.

Each member of the human race is human and therefore a "natural person." That is, every human being is a person by the mere fact of being human at whatever stage of physical, mental, spiritual, economic, or political stage of development. By virtue of this fact, each person has the capacity to organize and act directly on the common good. This is done not as an individual *per se*, but as a member of a group — although (and this is important) in a way in which he or she does not lose his or her individual identity or rights.

If we are faced with unjust structures that inhibit or prevent us from owning an adequate stake in the means of production sufficient to generate a living income, then we do not need to go, hat-in-hand, either to a rich private elite and beg for alms, or to the State and surrender our personal sovereignty in exchange for our vote and a bare sufficiency to meet our material needs. The only thing we need is a specific plan, for — without that — we might as well just stay where we are. If you don't know where you are going, any road will take you there . . . and rather quickly, at that.

Such a plan is Capital Homesteading, a concept embodied in a proposal called the "Capital Homestead Act."

The Capital Homestead Act is a modern version of Abraham Lincoln's 1862 Homestead Act that (usually — there were some exceptions) offered a quarter section of land (160 acres) on the frontier to anyone 21 years of age or over, and who was an American citizen or declared the intent to become one. While there are many modern critics blessed with 20/20 hindsight who can point out the flaws of the Homestead Act, it cannot be denied that the Act was the most successful economic initiative in American history, excepting only the fact of America itself.[1] The Homestead Act laid the foundation for America's rise as the world's greatest industrial power. The Act embedded ownership of the means of production as the road to economic and political independence deep in the American psyche. Even more than a century of effort by the State and other forces have been unable to root it out entirely.

Unfortunately, land has a singular and unique drawback. There is, generally, only so much to go around, and the land eventually runs out. There is, however, a frontier that, to all intents and purposes, cannot run out. That is the technological frontier, the sector of the productive economy made up of industrial and commercial enterprises.

Admittedly, hostility toward technology is also embedded deep in the American psyche. This is not because technology is evil, *per se*, but (as Hilaire Belloc pointed out in *The Servile State*, and Kelso and Adler a generation later), because the methods of corporate finance employed virtually guaranteed that ownership of the new technology would be concentrated in the hands of a very few people.[2] Since (as Daniel Webster observed in the Massachu-

---

[1] See Alexis de Tocqueville, *Democracy in America* (1835, 1840), as well as William Cobbett, *The Emigrant's Guide* (1829), available in an annotated edition from Economic Justice Media, ISBN 0-944997-01-5.

[2] "Had property been well distributed, protected by cooperative guilds, fenced round and supported by custom and by the autonomy of great artisan corporations, those accumulations of wealth, necessary for the launching of each new method of production and for each new perfection of it, would have been discovered in the mass of small owners. *Their* corporations, *their* little parcels of wealth combined would have furnished the capitalization required for the new processes, and men already owners would, as one invention succeeded another, have increased

setts Constitutional Convention of 1820), "power natu-rally and necessarily follows property," concentrated own-ership of the means of production automatically means concentrated power.

Americans hate concentrated power.

That's not to say that other people do not hate concen-trated power. There is, however, just something about the proud, the arrogant, those who exercise raw, naked power — as did the United States Supreme Court in *Roe v. Wade* — that excites a profound and visceral reaction in the American spirit. This aspect of the American spirit can only be ameliorated or all but extinguished through in-tensive and continuing — and State funded, of course — propaganda, and the fostering of a servile class ready, willing, and able to look to the State as the source of all that is good. This is in sharp contrast to what Alexis de Tocqueville observed in the early 19th century of the habit Americans had of organizing and taking care of matters themselves without the bumbling interference of the cen-tral government.

Nevertheless, despite the debilitating results of train-ing people to look to the State as the source of every bless-ing, the fire of the American spirit is not so easily extin-guished. Rather, the state of society in which we seem to be trapped today is the result of the fact that most Ameri-cans were never given a chance to share in the ownership

---

the total wealth of the community without disturbing the bal-ance of distribution. There is no conceivable link in reason or in experience which binds the capitalization of a new process with the idea of a few employing owners and a mass of employed nonowners working at a wage. Such great discoveries coming in a society like that of the thirteenth century would have blest and enriched mankind. Coming upon the diseased moral condi-tions of the eighteenth century in this country, they proved a curse." Hilaire Belloc, *The Servile State.* Section 4, "How the Distributive State Failed." Indianapolis, Indiana: Liberty Fund Classics, 1977, (100-101).

and profits of our high-tech industrial and commercial frontier, which (unlike land) has no known limits.

Capital Homesteading would take nothing away from present owners, who would be left with their current accumulations intact. They would only lose the virtual monopoly they now have over ownership of future capital.

By returning to a sound understanding of money, credit, and banking and employing advanced techniques of corporate finance, Capital Homesteading would link every American (especially the poorest of the poor and those previously economically disenfranchised) to the profits from sustainable economic growth. Every citizen could gain a share in power over technological progress and the tools and enterprises of modern society. Through widespread, direct ownership of the means of production everyone would participate in a more democratic economic process, just as they now participate in the democratic political process through access to the ballot.

The only question remaining is how Capital Homesteading would probably work — and why people seem to think it won't.

21. The Way Things Work

"It sounds nice, but . . ." — or so begin the usual rejoinders when people wish to evade their individual and personal responsibility to work for the common good, first within their immediate *milieux*, and — always — with an eye toward the effect that every act has on the common good as a whole. This is what is called a "well-formed social conscience." Despite such equivocations, however, all of the excuses given for not promoting Capital Homesteading as a Pro-Life economic agenda either fall apart from the pressure of their own contradictions, or are clearly evasions of responsibility. To take only two,

"'They' won't let us/you." What "they"? Who is this "they"? Please be specific! "They" is defined in the dictionary as "the generalized 'other'." A "generalized other" can do nothing. It takes a particular (that is, identifiable and specific) "other" to carry out an act as definite as preventing Capital Homesteading or anything else. What people usually mean when they say, "'they' won't let us/you," is that our social institutions are badly organized. If so, these institutions are inhibiting or preventing the practice of virtue, specifically, the acquisition and possession of private property in the means of production. That being the case, the solution (as Ferree made clear in *Introduction to Social Justice*) is to organize and carry out "acts of social justice" to restructure our institutions so that they once again assist us in our acquisition and development of virtue instead of operating to our detriment.

"It's impossible." It's astonishing how often something people don't want to do or don't understand is "impossible." It's impossible to have a stable society without a god-king. It's impossible to sail across the ocean-sea without falling off the edge of the earth. It's impossible for a remote and heterogeneous collection of colonies to unite

and break away from the mother country. It's impossible
to fly. It's impossible to go to the Moon.

On the contrary, as Ferree explained in *Introduction to
Social Justice*, "Another characteristic of Social Justice, . .
. is that in Social Justice there is never any such thing as
helplessness. No problem is ever too big or too complex, no
field is ever too vast, for the methods of this Social Justice. Problems that were agonizing in the past and were
simply dodged, even by serious and virtuous people, can
now be solved with ease by any school child."[1]

And so on. Excuses could be listed *ad nauseam*, but
what's the point? They are *excuses*, not reasons. The principles supporting Capital Homesteading have never been
successfully challenged despite decades of demands that
critics get explicit about what, exactly, is wrong with
them. The best anyone has ever been able to do is to
claim, based on *other* principles, that Capital Homesteading or the Just Third Way is crazy, stupid, evil, or some
other handy pejorative as helpful as it is scholarly. This,
of course, is much easier than actually arguing or thinking.

So, aside from panic-stricken excuses, injured pride,
and a general feeling of individual helplessness, there is
nothing to prevent a "Capital Homestead Act" from being
enacted. The only things remaining are to outline (briefly)
how Capital Homesteading works, and figure out where
the money is to come from. For the full-blown program, of
course, interested readers should go to *Capital Homesteading for Every Citizen* (2004). Because the question as
to where we are to get the money is of such paramount
importance, we will cover it first.

The "money question" is actually easy to answer, once
we understand a few basic concepts, the most important
of which is that "money" is anything that can be used in
settlement of a debt. The Capital Homestead Act proposes
a number of programs so that every man, woman and

---

[1] Ferree, *op. cit.*, 47.

child could get interest-free (though not "cost-free") capital credit from a local bank. The bank would create new money backed by the present value of the financially feasible project brought in for funding. Consistent with the tenets of the classic "Banking School" of finance and the real bills doctrine, future earnings of the capital purchased would pay off the loans, including bank service fees and premiums to cover capital credit default insurance and reinsurance. Every member of a family would get access to this special credit by setting up a tax-sheltered Capital Homestead Account (CHA) — like a "Super-IRA" — at a local bank or other financial institution.

It is critical to understand that no money is or can be created under Capital Homesteading until and unless a "financially feasible" capital project is brought to a commercial bank for financing. It is not a case of creating money, then spending it, as current government monetary policy and virtually all of academia insist is the way the financial system must operate. Instead, a sound investment is identified, properly vetted by the bank and the insurance company, and then — *and only then* — is the money created to loan to the "Capital Homesteader."

This is based on classic banking theory embodied in the real bills doctrine. Briefly, a commercial bank can create money — remember, defining "money" as anything that can be used in settlement of a debt — at will, without inflation or deflation. This, however, is only so long as the amount of money created does not exceed the present value of an existing asset or future stream of income from an asset to be financed. Backing for the money comes from taking a lien on the future asset to a bank for "discounting" (sale to the bank). The bank can itself obtain money by rediscounting the same lien at the central bank.

The piece of paper or other medium that conveys a lien (a legal claim to an asset — "a charge or security or incumbrance upon property"[2]) is called a "bill." If the bill represents something of actual, definable value, it is a "real bill." If it is fraudulent or represents something that does not have actual, definable (and verifiable) value, it is called a "fictitious bill." Having value, a real bill can be exchanged for something else having value, thereby functioning as "money."

---

[2] "Lien," *Black's Law Dictionary*.

22. *Own v. Wage*

An economic agenda for the Pro-Life movement sounds like a good idea, but it won't do any good if it doesn't work. Some people have asserted that the "Living (or Just) Wage" as described by Rev. John A. Ryan in his 1906 book, *A Living Wage,* is the only possible economic agenda for the Pro-Life movement. The serious flaws in the wage system, however, examined in detail by such diverse authorities as Karl Marx, Pope Leo XIII, G. K. Chesterton and Hilaire Belloc (the "Chesterbelloc"), and Louis Kelso and Mortimer Adler, as well as Msgr. Ryan himself[1] pretty much take any reliance on wages as the sole source of a viable living income out of the running.

We can therefore dismiss the two main systems that rely on the wage system: capitalism and socialism. The only real difference between the two is the identity of the small elite that owns or controls ownership of the means of production, anyway. What we propose, then, is something analogous to Chesterton and Belloc's "distributism," or an economic arrangement of society characterized by widespread direct ownership of the means of production.

Classic distributism adds that there is a preference (not a mandate) for small, family-owned farms and artisan shops. Further, Chesterton and Belloc assumed as a given that existing accumulations of savings are necessary to finance capital formation. The goal of widespread direct ownership of the means of production, however, is more important than the specific means used to achieve the goal — particularly if the means are contrary to sound principles of economics and finance, or somehow violate fundamental principles of the natural moral law.

---

[1] See, *e.g.,* Msgr. John A. Ryan, *Distributive Justice* (1916).

As we saw in the previous chapter, Capital Homesteading gets away from the presumed reliance on existing accumulations of savings to finance capital formation by
going back to sound banking principles. A commercial
bank that has the power to act as a "bank of issue" (that
is, can issue banknotes or create demand deposits —
checking accounts), can take a real bill — a lien on something of value — as security from a borrower. This is
backed up with a capital credit insurance policy for addi-
tional security, or "collateral." The bank can then print
banknotes or create a demand deposit in the amount
loaned on the bill, and hand the banknotes or checkbook
over to the borrower.

The borrower takes the "money" and invests it in a project that is reasonably expected to generate enough profit
to repay the loan, buy back the real bill, and provide sufficient income for the borrower on which to live. When the
loan is repaid, the bank cancels the banknotes or the demand deposit, and returns the bill to the borrower, who in
turn cancels the bill.

Because the money is created in the same or lesser
amount of the present value of the investment, there can
be no inflation unless the investment fails. In that case, of
course, the money supply is reduced by the amount of the
capital credit insurance proceeds paid to the lender. That
is, the inflationary effect of the failed investment is offset
by the deflationary effect of the lender canceling the insurance proceeds used to repay the loan. The capital
credit insurance company pays off on the policy, and the
bank takes the money and cancels the money, the way the
bank would have had the loan been repaid by the borrower in the usual way. This offsets the inflationary im-
pact of the prior money creation for the failed investment.

Thus, by getting the right to go to a commercial bank
and borrow up to, say, $7,000, and participate with the
bank in creating money in this fashion, a "Capital Homesteader" could, with the guidance of a competent financial
advisor, purchase part ownership in: 1) companies for

which a member of the family works; 2) a company where the Homesteader has a monthly billing account; or 3) "qualified" companies that are well-managed and highly profitable. Companies could also establish Employee Stock Ownership Plans (ESOPs) for their workers, and Consumer Stock Ownership Plans (CSOPs) for their regular customers to borrow funds repayable with future pre-tax profits, for the issuance of new shares, or for the purchase of existing shares.

Communities that adopt for-profit Citizens Land Cooperatives (CLCs) could attract interest-free credit to buy land for development or build new infrastructure. This would enable every citizen to participate as a shareholder in community land planning and governance decisions. Moreover, each citizen would share in the profits from rents and fees for the use of land and infrastructure. Through a Capital Homestead Act, access to capital credit — which today helps make the rich richer — would be enshrined in law as a fundamental right of citizenship, like the right to vote.

Using its powers under § 13 of the Federal Reserve Act of 1913, the Federal Reserve System would supply local commercial banks with the money needed by businesses to grow. The central bank would discount the real bills presented to commercial banks, instead of allowing banks to create money on their own. This would stabilize the currency and provide immediate 100% "hard asset" reserves for all the money in the commercial banking system.

An important feature of Capital Homesteading is that the new money and credit for private sector growth would flow through Capital Homestead Accounts and other credit democratization vehicles. This would ensure that as many people as possible had the means to acquire and possess private property in the means of production. Capital Homesteading would thereby enable a country to comply with the recommendation expressed by Pope Leo

XIII in what is generally considered the first "social encyclical," *Rerum Novarum,*

> We have seen that this great labor question cannot be solved save by assuming as a principle that private ownership must be held sacred and inviolable. The law, therefore, should favor ownership, and its policy should be to induce as many as possible of the people to become owners.[2]

Through a well-regulated central banking system and other safeguards (including capital credit insurance to cover the risk of bad loans), all citizens could purchase with interest-free capital credit, newly issued shares representing newly added machines and structures.[3] These purchases would be paid off with dividends that the paying companies could deduct from their taxable income. Nothing would come out of anyone's existing accumulations of savings or reduce the income anyone uses for consumption purposes.

Once the acquisition loan was fully repaid, the Capital Homesteader would be the full, legal owner of the shares. Thereafter, the Homesteader would receive an adequate and regular income sufficient to meet common domestic needs from the earnings of the capital he or she accumulated over the years, and be able to pass it on to any children.

That is how Capital Homesteading is designed to work — although we have only hinted at the technical details of the proposal. It only remains to organize in solidarity with like-minded others, and get to work. The first step would be to visit the CESJ website, www.cesj.org, and find out more about Capital Homesteading.

---

[2] Pope Leo XIII, *Rerum Novarum* ("On Labor and Capital"), 1891, § 46.

[3] http://www.cesj.org/socialsecurity/safeguards-cha.html

Conclusion

As we have discovered in our examination of the question of how to transform the economy from life support to supporting life, the belief that abortion is a constitutionally protected right is both the Pro-Choice movement's greatest strength and, paradoxically, its greatest weakness. No one can claim a right to choose to have, materially assist in procuring, or support abortion without at the same time acknowledging the right of others to choose *not* to have, materially assist in procuring, or support abortion.

If some people are denied the right to choose in order to secure the right of choice to others, then the presumed right to choose abortion is not, strictly speaking, a true right, but (just as Justice Bryan White declared) an exercise of raw judicial power — an act of tyranny by means of which one group forces its will on another group or groups; not "right/duty," but "privilege/no right."[1] The Pro-Life movement can therefore justly demand that all forms of government support for abortion cease immediately — or force the Pro-Choice movement to admit that the alleged choice they themselves are demanding applies only to them, and is not, in fact, a right at all (which implies the functioning of justice), but the creation of a privileged class or establishment of a State religion that has been granted the power to rob the taxpayer for its own benefit.

Still, useful and effective as removal of all federal, state, and local government support for abortion would be, it is clearly not enough. Abortions took place long before anyone had the idea that there was any kind of right involved, or even before there was any kind of State sub-

---

[1] See Wesley Hohfeld's *Fundamental Legal Conceptions* (1919).

sidy or support. Once all government support for abortion has been eliminated, then, two things remain to be done.

First, people must be educated to realize that the fetus is a human being, is thus a person, and is thereby entitled to the full spectrum of natural rights that necessarily accompany the human condition. The Pro-Life movement has been perfecting its techniques in this effort since 1973. Considering the massive amounts of money spent by the Pro-Choice movement and the government support the Pro-Choice movement enjoys, the Pro-Life movement has been astonishingly successful. Nothing should be done to decrease current efforts.

A good case can and should be made that efforts must, on the contrary, increase dramatically. No day should pass without continuous protests outside any and all facilities providing abortions; no magazine or newspaper should be without its educational Pro-Life advertisement or article; prime time radio and television, as well as the internet, should carry the maximum possible amount of both informational and educational advertising. Denial of media access should be the basis for a lawsuit on the grounds of denial of free speech.

People in the Pro-Life movement might want to consider refusing to take even legitimate tax deductions for contributions for Pro-Life purposes. While any legal justification for denying tax deductibility is shaky — many Pro-Choice advocates claim to support the aims of the Pro-Life movement other than an end to abortion, and it is highly questionable whether even the United States Supreme Court would move to so abridge or discourage freedom of speech — such a move would be another great moral victory at a relatively small cost. Most people who contribute to Pro-Life organizations or causes do not consider the tax effects in any event. Voluntarily surrendering a legitimate tax deduction removes the possibility that the Pro-Life movement would be labeled hypocritical for demanding an end to tax deductions for contributions to

Pro-Choice organizations or causes, while continuing to take advantage of them to present an opposing view.

Whatever the motivation, the Pro-Life movement now has the opportunity to gain a great victory, simply by insisting that the principles on which the Pro-Choice movement claims to base its position be applied consistently, fairly, and in justice. Either Pro-Choice adherents acquiesce in the demand that all forms of government support for abortion, financial and otherwise, cease immediately, or the Pro-Choice movement loses all credibility and every vestige of a claim to be based on justice.

Anyone interested in promoting a Pro-Life economic agenda — and, incidentally, a possible way out of the current Great Recession (a.k.a., "The Jobless Recovery") — should look over the material on the CESJ website, and consider in what way he or she could advance the effort. As we said in the opening section of this book, only in this way can we get the economy and the whole of society off of life support, and begin the task of supporting life. One of the better ways this can be done is to spread the word, and open doors to "prime movers" such as Barack Obama who might be open to hearing about something that has the promise to deliver justice instead of inflation, joblessness, war, poverty, and death.

Bibliography

Articles, Papers, and Other Documents

Adler, Mortimer, "The Meaning of Natural Law."

Allen, Charlotte, "Justice for All: A Class in Ethical Sudoku," *The Wall Street Journal*, 10/09/09, W13.

Kurland, Norman G., "A New Look at Prices and Money: The Kelsonian Binary Model for Achieving Rapid Growth Without Inflation," *The Journal of Socio-Economics*, Vol. 30, 495-515.

Leo XIII, *Rerum Novarum* ("On Capital and Labor"), 1891.

Pius XI, *Quadragesimo Anno* ("On the Restructuring of the Social Order"), 1931.

Pius XI *Divini Redemptoris* ("On Atheistic Communism"), 1937.

Books

Aquinas, Thomas, *De Regimine Principum*. Toronto, Canada: St. Michael's College, 1935.

Aquinas, Thomas, *Summa Theologica*. Westminster, Maryland: Christian Classics, 1981.

Aristotle, *The Politics*. London: Penguin Books, 1981.

Ashford, Robert, and Shakespeare, Rodney, *Binary Economics: The New Paradigm*. Lanham, Maryland. University Press of America, 1999.

Bellarmine, Robert, *De Laicis, or, The Treatise on Civil Government*. New York: Fordham University Press, 1928.

Belloc, Hilaire, *The Servile State*. Indianapolis, Indiana, Liberty Fund, Inc., 1977.

Black's Law Dictionary. St. Paul, Minnesota: West Publishing Company, 1951.

Chesterton, G. K., *Saint Thomas Aquinas: "The Dumb Ox."* New York: Doubleday Image Books, 1956.

Chesterton, G. K., *The Outline of Sanity. Volume V, Collected Works*. San Francisco, California: Ignatius Press, 1987.

Cobbett, William, *The Emigrant's Guide*. Arlington, Virginia: Economic Justice Media, 2008.

Ferree, William J., S.M., Ph.D., *Introduction to Social Justice*. Arlington, Virginia: Center for Economic and Social Justice, 1997.

108

SUPPORTING LIFE

Fisher, Irving, "National Vitality, Its Wastes and Conservation." Vol. 3 of the Report of the National Conservation Commission issued in 1909 as Senate document no. 676, 60th Congress, 2d Session.

Greaney, Michael D., *Social Justice Betrayed*. St. Louis, Missouri: Central Bureau, Catholic Central Union of America, 2000.

Greaney, Michael D., *In Defense of Human Dignity, Essays on the Just Third Way: A Natural Law Perspective*. Arlington, Virginia: Economic Justice Media, 2008.

Kelso, Louis O., and Adler, Mortimer J., *The Capitalist Manifesto*. New York: Random House, 1958.

Kelso, Louis O., and Adler, Mortimer J., *The New Capitalists*. New York: Random House, 1961.

Kurland, Norman G., Brohawn, Dawn K., and Greaney, Michael D., *Capital Homesteading for Every Citizen*. Arlington, Virginia: Economic Justice Media, 2004.

Lewis, C. S., *The Abolition of Man*. New York: Harper Collins, 2001.

Maritain, Jacques, *The Person and the Common Good*. Notre Dame, Indiana: University of Notre Dame Press, 1966.

Marx, Karl and Engels, Friedrich, *The Communist Manifesto*. London: Penguin Books, 1967.

Miyamoto Musashi, *A Book of Five Rings*. New York: Barnes and Noble, 1997.

Mounier, Emmanuel, *A Personalist Manifesto*. London: Longmans, Green and Co., 1938.

Rommen, Heinrich, *The Natural Law*. Indianapolis, Indiana: Liberty Fund, Inc., 1998.

Ryan, Rev. John A., *A Living Wage*. New York: Macmillan, 1906.

Say, Jean-Baptiste, *Letters to Mr. Malthus*. London: Sherwood, Neely & Jones, 1821.

Schumpeter, Joseph A., *History of Economic Analysis*. New York: Oxford University Press, 1954.

Sun Tzu, *The Art of War*. New York: Oxford University Press, 1963.

Tocqueville, Alexis de, *Democracy in America*. New York: Alfred A. Knoph, 1945.

Williams, Howard R., *Cases and Materials on the Law of Property*. Brooklyn, New York: The Foundation Press, Inc., 1954.

Index

savings, future, 86
savings, past, 85, 86
Say, Jean-Baptiste, 85
Servile State, The, 63, 88,
  92, 107
slavery, 37, 61, 62, 66, 85
slaves, 15, 39, 62, 66
Smith, Adam, 85
social order, 12, 18, 51, 53,
  57, 65, 66, 71, 75, 76
socialism, 11, 14, 15, 62, 87,
  89, 99
Sun Tzu, 3, 108
Supreme Court of the
  United States, 35, 37,
  39-45, 48, 49, 58, 66, 78,
  83, 93, 104
technology, 87, 88, 92

Third Reich, 44, 45
Tocqueville, Alexis de, 48,
  52, 92, 93, 108
Torah, 26, 29
United States, 1, 35-37, 40-
  45, 48-53, 66, 73, 79, 83,
  93, 104
Virtue, 72
Wall Street Journal, 18, 107
Wealth of Nations, The, 85
Webster, Daniel, 92
Weismann, Dr. Max,
  President, Center for the
  Study of the Great Ideas,
  1, 19-21
White, Justice Bryan, 49,
  103
William of Occam, 30